Saved from the grave: Neolithic to Saxon discoveries at Spring Road Municipal Cemetery, Abingdon, Oxfordshire, 1990–2000

By T G Allen and Z Kamash

with contributions by

Leigh Allen, Alistair Barclay, Alister Bartlett, Paul Blinkhorn, Paul Booth, Ceridwen Boston, Angela Boyle, Diane Briscoe, M G Canti, Bethan Charles, Peter Hacking, Martin Henig, Tom Higham, Jonathan Hiller, Hugo Lamdin-Whymark, Peter Marshall, Mark Nokkert, Peter Northover, J van der Plicht, Mark Robinson, R Sparks, Jane Timby, Rachel Tyson

Illustrations by

Peter Lorimer, Rosalyn Lorimer, Sarah Lucas, Simon Pressey, Anne Stewardson

Oxford Archaeology
Thames Valley Landscape Monograph No. 28
2008

The publication of this volume has been generously funded by English Heritage

Published for Oxford Archaeology by Oxford University School of Archaeology as part of the Thames Valley Landscapes Monograph series

Designed by Oxford Archaeology Graphics Office

Summarised and Edited by Chris Hayden

This book is part of a series of books about the Thames Valley Landscapes – which can be bought from all good bookshops and Internet Bookshops. For more information visit thehumanjourney.net

ISBN 978-0-9549627-6-0

Typeset and printed in Europe by the Alden Group, Oxfordshire

Contents

Contents

List of Figures

List of Plates

List of Tables

Summary

Excavations and salvage recording carried out within the Spring Gardens municipal cemetery over the last fifty years have revealed evidence of archaeological activity from the Mesolithic to the Saxon period. Situated on a gravel rise alongside the Larkhill Stream, occasional struck flints indicate that the site was visited by Mesolithic hunter-gatherers, and a few sherds of early Neolithic pottery show that the first farmers also visited. The location apparently became more important in the middle and late Neolithic periods, as shown by a Peterborough Ware vessel and a Grooved Ware pit, and by an early Beaker burial accompanied by a copper awl. Sherds of early Bronze Age pottery suggest that the site continued to be significant to the local community during this period, and in the middle Bronze Age an arc of substantial postholes probably indicates the construction of a timber circle, one of very few of this date in southern Britain. This was accompanied by various pits or postholes, and a scattering of similar features was also present in the late Bronze Age.

The early to middle Iron Age saw the erection of a substantial timber roundhouse, at whose centre was a pit, and within whose circumference a group of three middle Iron Age crouched burials was found, formally deposited in purpose-dug graves. Other undated crouched burials were present across the site, possibly indicating a dispersed cemetery. There was otherwise little evidence of middle or late Iron Age activity, but in the Roman period ditched or fenced enclosures were laid out and the site was used for domestic occupation in the 2nd and 3rd centuries AD. The site was reoccupied in the 6th century AD, when a variety of Saxon features including sunken-featured buildings and ditches were dug, but it is unclear whether the occupation continued into the 7th century AD. In the 13th century the east side of the site was used for gravel extraction, possibly relating to the construction of a chapel and cemetery at the adjacent road junction, but thereafter the area became part of the arable fields of Abingdon. At the turn of the 19th–20th centuries the area again became a gravel pit, and this extended into the north-east corner of the site. The quarry was short-lived, and the site reverted to open ground used for pasture until taken over for burials in 1940.

Zusammenfassung

Aus- und Notgrabungen, die auf dem Gelände des Gemeindefriedhofs von Spring Gardens in den letzten fünfzig Jahren durchgeführt wurden, enthüllten archäologische Zeugnisse, welche vom Mesolithikum bis hin in die Sachsenzeit reichen.

Auf einer Kiesanhebung entlang des Flusses Larkhill gelegen, deuten gelegentliche Flintabschläge darauf hin, dass die Stelle von mesolithischen Jägern und Sammlern besucht wurde. Des weiteren geben Funde einiger Neolithischer Keramikscherben darauf Aufschluss, dass auch die ersten Ackerbauern den Standort aufsuchten. Vermutlich stieg die Bedeutung der Fundstelle im mittleren und späten Neolithikum, was durch Peterborough Ware Gefäßfunde, einer Grooved Ware Grube und frühen Beaker Bestattungen denen Pfriemen beigegeben waren unterstrichen wird.

Frühbronzezeitliche Tonscherben deuten darauf hin, dass der Fundplatz auch während dieser Zeitperiode eine wichtige Rolle für die kommunale Gemeinschaft gewesen sein muss. Aus der mittleren Bronzezeit ist eine bogenförmige Anreihung großer Pfostenlöcher bekannt, die scheinbar auf die Konstruktion eines Holzkreises hindeutet, einem von nur sehr wenigen, welche aus dieser Zeit in Britannien bekannt sind. Der Kreis wurde begleitet von verschiedenen Gruben und Pfostenlöchern, eine ähnliche Ansammlung solcher Befunde ist auch aus der späten Bronzezeit bekannt.

Die frühe bis mittlere Bronzezeit sah die Errichtung eines enormen Rundhauses, in dessen Mittelpunkt eine Grube plaziert war. In ihrer Peripherie wurde eine Gruppe von drei Hockerbestattungen gefunden. Diese Gräber wurden zweifelsohne formell und einzig für den Zweck der Bestattung ausgehoben.

Weitere undatierte Hockerbestattungen wurden überall auf dem Gelände verzeichnet, diese könnten möglicherweise auf ein weit zerstreutes Gräberfeld hinweisen. Ansonsten gab es nur wenige Indizien auf mittlere- oder späteisenzeitliche Aktivitäten.

In der Römerzeit, im 2. und 3. nachchristlichen Jahrhundert, wurden Bereiche der Fundstelle durch Gräben und Zäune eingegrenzt und es ist von einem häuslichen Gebrauch der Fläche auszugehen.

Im 6. Jahrhundert kommt es zu einer Wiederbewohnung und eine Auswahl sächsischer Befunde, unter anderem abgesenkte Gebäude und Gräben, konnten nachgewiesen werden. Es bleibt jedoch unklar, ob die Besiedlung sich bis in das 7. Jahrhundert fortsetzte.

Im 13. Jahrhundert wurde die Ostseite der Fläche als Kiesgrube genutzt, eventuell in Verbindung mit dem Bau einer Kapelle und eines Friedhofs bei der benachbarten Straßenkreuzung. Nach dieser Zeit wurde die Grabungsfläche Teil der landwirtschaftlich genutzten Felder von Abingdon.

Am Übergang vom 19. zum 20. Jahrhundert wurde das Land erneut als Kiesgrube genutzt, diesmal jedoch einschließlich der nordöstlichen Ecke. Die Abbaugrube wurde nach kurzer Zeit geschlossen und von da an wurde das Gelände als Viehweide verwendet, bis es schließlich 1940 zum Gemeindefriedhof wurde.

Markus Dylewski

Résumé

Au cours des cinquante dernières années, les opérations d'archéologie préventives effectuées dans le cimetière municipal de Spring Gardens ont révélé l'existence de vestiges remontant du Mésolithique à la période Saxonne.

La découverte sporadique de silex en amont de la gravière qui jouxte la rivière Larkhill y atteste la présence de chasseurs-cueilleurs au Mésolithique et celle de tessons de poteries, l'installation d'une communauté agricole au Néolithique Ancien. Le site semble toutefois avoir pris une véritable importance à partir du Néolithique Moyen et Final, ce dont témoignent un récipient de type *Peterborough ware* et une fosse où l'on a découvert de la céramique de type *Grooved ware* (typiques du Néolithique Tardif britannique) et une sépulture du Campaniforme Ancien renfermant, entre autres, une alène en cuivre. D'autres tessons de céramiques confirment l'occupation du site jusqu'au Bronze Moyen. Par ailleurs, la mise au jour d'un ensemble de trous de poteaux contemporains de ces tessons démontre l'existence d'un enclos circulaire, un des rares du genre pour cette période dans le sud de l'Angleterre. L'édifice jouxtait vraisemblablement d'autres constructions comme le laissent supposer une série de fosses variées, de trous de poteaux ainsi qu'un ensemble épars de faits similaires datés entre le Bronze Moyen et le Bronze Récent. Entre le Premier et le Deuxième Age du Fer, ce site accueille un édifice circulaire renfermant en son centre une fosse à triple inhumation d'accroupis directement creusée dans le sol. La découverte d'autres sépultures de même type, non datées, confirme la vocation funéraire du site. Toutefois, seuls quelques vestiges épars semblent attester une activité sur le site à l'Age du Fer Récent. La période romaine, elle, se caractérise par l'érection d'enclos, en fossés ou en palissades. Aux II et IIIè siècles, le site a une vocation clairement domestique. Au VIè siècle, il est à nouveau occupé. Les divers vestiges de la période saxonne qui y ont été exhumés consistent notamment en des fosses et en édifices construits à un niveau inférieur à celui du sol naturel. Il n'est en revanche pas certain que cette occupation perdure au-delà du VIIè siècle.

Au XIIIè siècle, la portion Est du site sert à l'extraction du gravier. Cette exploitation est très certainement liée à la construction de la chapelle et du cimetière, situés à la jonction de routes adjacente. Par la suite, l'ensemble du site est exploité à des fins agricoles et devient une partie des terres arables d'Abingdon. Au tournant des XIX et XXè siècles, on y extrait à nouveau le gravier, de l'est au nord-est. La carrière n'a pas subsisté, le site ayant une fois encore été transformé en terres agricoles. Ce n'est qu'à partir de 1940 qu'il a de nouveau servi de cimetière.

Magali Bailliot
Nathalie Haudecoeur-Wilks

Acknowledgements

Oxford Archaeology is extremely grateful to English Heritage for funding this project. In particular we would like to acknowledge the assistance of English Heritage Inspectors Tony Fleming and Rob Perrin and Chief Archaeologist David Miles for the fieldwork, and Helen Keeley for her help with the post-excavation process. We are also indebted to Abingdon Town Council for giving permission to excavate, and would like to thank Brian Tonkin, formerly Clerk to Abingdon Town Council, for his co-operation. At the cemetery the support of successive superintendents John Bell and Richard Kell, and the information provided by Bill Skellington from retirement, is gratefully acknowledged.

The excavations were carried out by a mixture of professional and amateur archaeologists, all of whom we would like to thank. Martin Hicks supervised the 1990 evaluation, ably assisted by Jeff Parsons, and the 1994 excavations by the Abingdon society were run by Alison Gledhill and Roger Ainslie. The 2000 excavations were directed by Tim Allen, and managed on-site by Jonathan Hiller, who also wrote much of the post excavation assessment. The support of all the volunteers who took part is gratefully acknowledged.

We would also like to thank Alison Roberts, Arthur MacGregor and Julie Clements at the Ashmolean Museum, Lauren Gilmour at the Oxfordshire County Museums Store at Standlake and Cherry Grey at Abingdon Museum for their assistance in locating and loaning finds from the earlier excavations for analysis during post-excavation. We would also like to acknowledge the part played by David Brown and Tania Dickinson (formerly of the Ashmolean Museum and the Institute of Archaeology at Oxford respectively) in attempting to trace the Saxon pottery given by Bill Skellington.

The authors would like to thank all the contributors to the report. For the illustrations we would like to thank Peter and Rosalyn Lorimer; the flint illustrations were drawn by Simon Pressey. We are particularly grateful to Chris Hayden of Oxford Archaeology for summarising much of the full text for publication. The volume was copy edited by Ian Scott of Oxford Archaeology.

Chapter 1:   Introduction

by Tim Allen

LOCATION, GEOLOGY AND TOPOGRAPHY

Spring Road municipal cemetery (Fig. 1; Pl. 1) is situated in Abingdon, Oxfordshire (SU 4875 9755), north-west of the town centre, on Summertown-Radley 2nd gravel terrace deposits (BGS 1971). The gravel terrace deposits on which Abingdon lies are divided by a series of streams flowing south into the rivers Ock and Thames. The site itself is bounded on the west and north by the valley of the Larkhill Stream, while to the south the terrace dips gradually to Kimmeridge Clay deposits and, beyond that, to 1st terrace floodplain gravels adjacent to the river Ock some 400 m away. Only on the east is the gravel terrace uninterrupted, and the site thus occupies a slight eminence (BGS 1971).

To the north the site is bounded by houses built between the 1st and 2nd World Wars, and on the east by housing added after the 2nd World War (Pl. 1). To the west of the site are the levelled playing fields of Larkmead School and to the south is the previous municipal cemetery situated between Cemetery Road and Spring Gardens.

The site has been used for burials since 1940 and is landscaped and divided into numbered blocks (Fig. 2). The areas still unused for burials at the time of the excavations comprised blocks 8, 9 and 5.

CIRCUMSTANCES OF THE PROJECT

The Spring Road municipal cemetery is owned by Abingdon Town Council, who purchased the land before the Second World War and converted previously agricultural land into a cemetery in 1940. The depth and close spacing of the graves meant that most archaeological features within the boundary of the cemetery were destroyed. As the site fell outside the PPG16 planning framework, and in the light of significant finds made during grave-digging, Tim Allen of the Oxford Archaeological Unit (OAU) approached English Heritage and the town council in 1990 for funds to record the remaining undisturbed areas of the site ahead of the gradual expansion of the cemetery population, and English Heritage provided funds for an evaluation (Fig. 2; OAU 1990). In 1994 the Abingdon Area Archaeological and Historical Society (AAAHS) dug several small trenches (Fig. 2; Ainslie 1999a), but the society did not wish to commit itself to a long-running campaign of excavations. By 2000 modern burial had filled much of the cemetery. An area of c 3500 m^2 remained unused for burial. In the summer of 2000 the OAU was commissioned by English Heritage (with the co-operation of Abingdon Town Council) to undertake archaeological excavations (OAU 2000). The excavations were preceded by a geophysical survey of the unused part of the cemetery and part of the immediately adjacent sports field (Figs 41–42). Excavation took place within Areas 8 and 9 at the east side of the cemetery and in Area 5 in the north-west corner (Fig. 2).

ARCHAEOLOGICAL AND HISTORICAL BACKGROUND OF THE AREA

Prehistoric

The town lies in an area rich in archaeological remains of all periods (Fig. 1), and has seen human occupation and settlement for at least five and a half thousand years. North-east of the town at Daisy Banks, Radley, lay a causewayed enclosure with an associated earthen long mound (Case and Whittle 1982; Bradley 1984). South-west of the river Ock was another complex of monuments: a cursus, a long mortuary enclosure and a long barrow (Benson and Miles, 1974, 61–2, map 33; Ainslie and Wallis, 1987; Gledhill and Wallis, 1989; Barclay *et al.* 2003). Another long barrow has been identified from aerial photographs near Tesco's, west of Abingdon, only 1 km south-west of Spring Road, and has recently been evaluated (OAU 1997).

Evidence of late Neolithic activity was found east of the causewayed enclosure at Daisy Banks (Barclay and Halpin 1999). A pit containing Grooved Ware was excavated during the construction of the A34 just west of the Tesco's long barrow (Parrington 1978, fig. 25), and a Class II henge was found south of the Ock close to the Thames at Corporation Farm (Henderson in Barclay *et al.* 2003).

The Neolithic monument complexes later became foci for Beaker and Bronze Age barrow cemeteries. The linear barrow cemetery at Barrow Hills, east of Daisy Banks, Radley, is the best known (Barclay and Halpin 1999). Groups of round barrows are present, however, all around Abingdon, one group close to the Class II henge at Corporation Farm (Benson and Miles 1974, Map 33) and another to the north-west, one of which was excavated at Saxton Road (Leeds and Harden 1936). Further round barrows are located just north of the Ock, grouped around the long barrow south of Tesco's. Beakers have also been found outside the barrows in a recent evaluation of this site (OAU 1997). Closer to Spring Road, two ring-ditches were excavated at Ashville Trading Estate (Parrington 1978, 24–28) and further ring-ditches show as cropmarks c 400 m north-east of Spring Road at Barrow Field (Benson and Miles 1974, 57–8, map 30). Beaker pottery has also been recovered from the town centre (Wilson and Wallis 1991, 4; Allen 1990, 73).

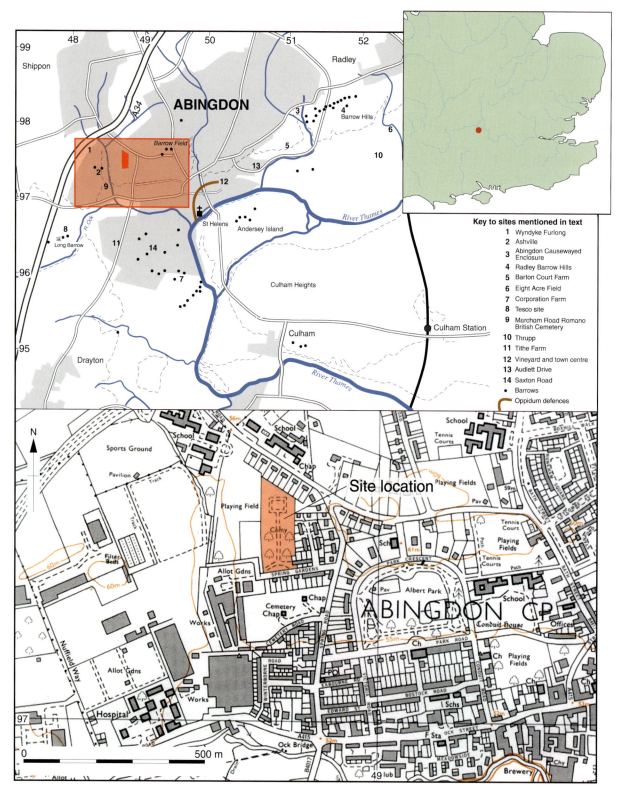

Figure 1   Site location.

Evidence of the later Bronze Age is focussed in two areas, one west and one east of Abingdon. On the west, the evidence comprises a middle Bronze Age enclosure at Corporation Farm (Shand *et al.* 2003), a waterhole south of Tesco (OAU 1997) and cremations at Ashville (Parrington 1978). On the east

there are cremations at Barrow Hills, Radley (Barclay and Halpin 1999, 167) and a field system at Eight Acre Field, Radley (Mudd 1995). There is also late Bronze Age activity at the latter site, and there are two late Bronze Age inhumations in earlier burial monuments at Barrow Hills.

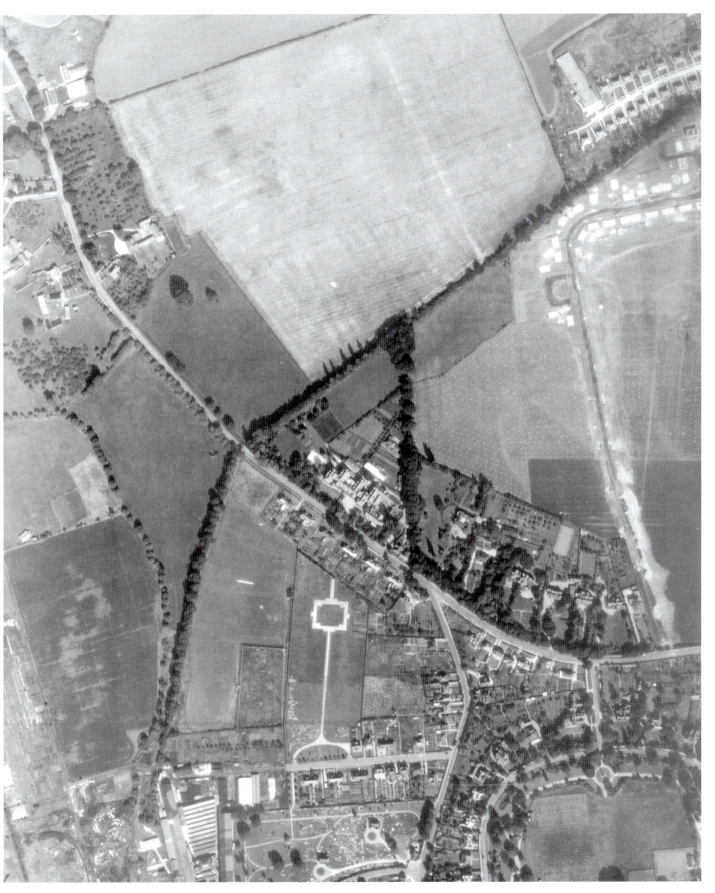

Plate 1   Aerial photograph of the site in 1951.

An extensive early and middle Iron Age settlement lay just west of the Larkhill Stream only a few hundred metres from Spring Road, and has been excavated at Ashville Trading Estate and Wyndyke Furlong (Parrington 1978; Muir and Roberts 1999). Traces of another middle Iron Age settlement have been found at Tithe Farm south of the river Ock (Ainslie 1992b). A large early and middle Iron Age settlement lay beneath the present town centre (Miles 1975; Jones 1983; Allen 1990) and another early Iron Age site lay south of Audlett Drive (Keevill 1992; OAU 1998). East of the town further settlement evidence has been recovered, notably at Thrupp (Wallis 1981; Everett and Eeles 1999) and at Barton Court Farm (Miles 1986).

Late Iron Age and Roman

By the late Iron Age, a native *oppidum* was established at Abingdon, defended with two or three ditches and an internal bank, which continued as a market-centre in the early Roman period (Allen 1991; 1993a; 1995; 1997). In the 2nd century it developed into a small town spreading beyond the defences (Thomas unpublished; Allen 1994; 1996), with substantial buildings (Thomas unpublished; Allen 1990; Wilson and Wallis 1991, J Moore pers. comm.), and cemeteries or burials immediately adjacent on the north-west, north and east sides (Atkinson and McKenzie 1946; Atkinson 1947; Ainslie 1995; Wilson 1979; OAU 1998). The later Roman levels have been severely truncated by medieval and more recent housing development within the town, but the quantity of pottery and coins show that the town continued to flourish until the very end of the 4th century.

Villas such as that at Barton Court Farm (Miles 1986) were the centres of rural estates, and while no estate centre has been confirmed west of the town, ditches, wells and other features have been identified at Ashville Trading Estate and Wyndyke Furlong (Parrington 1978; Muir and Roberts 1999). A small late Roman cemetery is recorded close to Marcham Road (Parrington 1978, 23–5) to the south-west, and the site of a building, interpreted as a temple, lies at Tithe Farm, south of the river Ock (Brown 1968, 137; Benson and Miles 1974, 57–8, map 30). A Roman building has also been recorded to the west of Saxton Road cemetery (Benson and Miles 1974).

Anglo-Saxon, medieval and post-medieval

Within the town two *Grubenhäuser* of 5th-century date were found during excavations in The Vineyard. Saxon loomweights have also been found in the High Street and Boxhill Walk, north of the town centre (Allen 1990; Rodwell 1975; A Dodd pers. comm.).

West of Abingdon and south of the river Ock at Saxton Road a large Saxon cemetery containing over 200 mixed inhumations and cremations was excavated in 1934 (Leeds and Harden 1936; Myres 1968; Myres 1977). The cemetery began in the 5th century, providing evidence of early penetration by the

Anglo-Saxons up the Thames similar to that at Dorchester (Chadwick Hawkes 1986, 69–71). This may have been the burial-place of the Saxon community at Corporation Farm, Drayton (Benson and Miles 1974, 61–3 map 33), but probably also contains burials from the settlement in the town centre. Finds from Wyndyke Furlong west of the Larkhill stream suggest some Saxon activity, although no settlement was located (Muir and Roberts 1999, fig. 3.7). South of the town there was a significant Saxon complex at Drayton and Sutton Courtenay (Hamerow *et al.* in prep.), but west of this very little material has come to light through recent evaluation (Hearne 2000), suggesting that Saxon settlement was focused close to the Thames itself.

Just east of the town centre at Audlett Drive a settlement of sunken huts and posthole buildings was found (Keevill 1992). Further north-east at Radley, Barrow Hills, a large settlement consisting of sunken huts and posthole timber buildings has been excavated (Chambers and Halpin 1986; Chambers and McAdam 2007.), and a smaller settlement of the same type was excavated at Barton Court Farm (Miles 1986), probably an outlier of the Barrow Hills settlement.

The early medieval abbey was founded in *c* 675 on the site of an earlier pagan settlement (Rodwell 1975, 33). The church of St Helens is supposed to have originated as a sister foundation that did not last, but the church survived as a minster serving a very large area (Blair 1994, 64–8). The abbey was sacked by the Danes and was refounded in the 10th century. The abbey came to dominate the town's affairs, and in the medieval period a large number of chapels were founded including two at opposite ends of Ock Bridge. Another chapel may have been located at the junction of Spring Road and Faringdon Road, where a small medieval cemetery is known (Harman and Wilson 1981; Chambers and Fuller 1986). Rocque's map of Berkshire shows that there was previously a triangle of land at the road junction here, and this may have been the site of a wayside chapel, or perhaps a gallows (Plate 9).

Munby has mapped the relationship of the town and its parishes to the medieval three-field system: the Spring Road site lies between 'Hitching Field' and a north-south strip known as Lower Furlong immediately west of Upper Lark Hill (Munby in Lambrick and Slade 1991, fig. 4). In the post-medieval period this area continued to be agricultural, as maps of the 18th and 19th centuries show. The 2nd edition Ordnance Survey 6″ map of 1900 (and that of 1904) shows that a small gravel pit was in operation west of the Spring Road junction with Faringdon Road, and the southern end of this appears to have extended into the cemetery site. The area between Spring Road and the Larkhill Stream was incorporated into the suburban development of Abingdon in the 20th century, and the plot of land now occupied by the cemetery is visible on the Ordnance Survey 6″ map of 1938, although the site was not used as a municipal cemetery until 1940.

N

55

Tr F

Tr 4

5

39
31

6

A

14

20

7

A

P

P

32

31

4

20

1

A

P

Tr E

8

32

Tr 3

Tr D

Post medieval burial

Tr C

9

3

Tr 2

Tr 1

Tr B

1

A

P

32

32

2

10

1

A

P

1

P

31

A

14

1

P

A

11

M

B

Tr A

1

C

10 Cemetery block

— Graves containing finds

— Approximate locations
of ancient graves

Oxford Archaeology
Assesment Trenches 1990

Abingdon Archaeological
Society Trenches 1994/5

Excavated areas 2000

0   50 m

Westfields

Spring Gardens

Figure 2   Plan of excavation areas, showing cemetery layout and plot numbering.

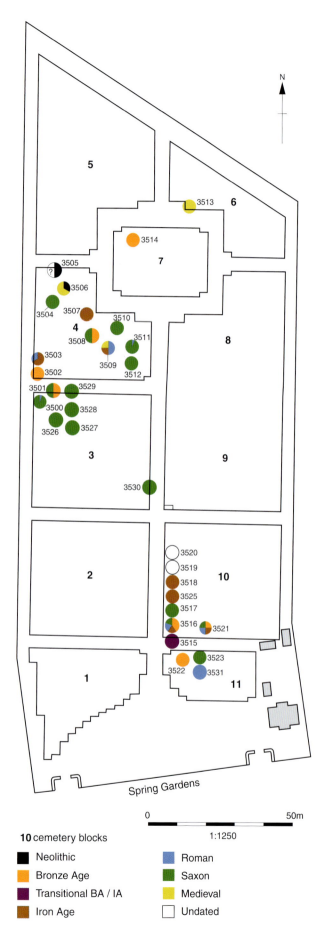

10 cemetery blocks

⬛ Neolithic	🟦 Roman
🟧 Bronze Age	🟩 Saxon
🟪 Transitional BA / IA	🟨 Medieval
🟫 Iron Age	⬜ Undated

PREVIOUS ARCHAEOLOGY OF THE SPRING ROAD CEMETERY

No records were kept of the any finds from the earliest graves in the south-west part of the cemetery (most of plots 1 and 2). The first recorded discoveries were of two extended inhumations in one grave, heads to the north, from the north end of cemetery plot 2, reported by a Dr O'Connell to the Ashmolean Museum in the 1950s (Case 1957, 104). In 1962 Bill Skellington, a keen amateur archaeologist, became Cemetery Superintendent, and recorded finds of a variety of periods. These included struck flints and Beaker pottery (Gray 1972, 238; Ashmolean Museum Acc. No. 1971.21-3), and Saxon pottery (eg Berisford 1973, fig. 39.6–8). Skeletons found by Bill Skellington were re-interred in modern graves; bones found in the 1950s, before Bill Skellington's appointment, were kept at the Superintendent's office, but were re-interred at the site before Bill Skellington retired.

Much other material was kept at the Superintendent's office, and Mr Skellington's successor, John Bell, continued to curate and add to this collection. Some of this material, including a largely complete late Bronze Age fine-ware bowl (Fig. 31, 1) and early Iron Age pottery is now held by the County Museums Service (Accession No. 1994.29). Many finds have been precisely located as a result of careful recording (Figs 2 and 3).

The 1990 evaluation comprised six trenches (Fig. 2, A-F) which showed that Iron Age and Roman features including gullies and postholes were present in the eastern part of the cemetery. Saxon occupation was inferred from lines of postholes, from a possible sunken-featured building, and from an occupation layer which contained a sherd of Saxon pottery and seemed to seal Roman ditches (OAU 1990). Owing to the substantial build up of soil in this part of the site, the remains were well-preserved.

In the face of continuing burial, the AAAHS excavated four test pits in 1994–5, mostly near to the site of the trenches previously excavated by OAU (Fig. 2). Gullies and postholes were found together with pottery of Iron Age, Roman and Saxon date (Ainslie 1999a). In 1999 grave diggers found a crouched inhumation in cemetery plot 5 in the north-west part of the site (Fig. 2). OAU made a brief record of the burial, but there were no directly associated finds and no bone was retained for dating.

LOCATION OF THE ARCHIVE

The finds from the 1990, 1994 and 2000 excavations, together with the paper archive and a copy of the digital data, have been deposited with the Oxfordshire County Museums Service at Standlake, Oxon. Some of the finds made by Bill Skellington and

Figure 3 Distribution map of gravediggers' finds with indication dated finds.

others were donated to the Ashmolean Museum in the 1960s, and remain within their collection. A copy of the digital data has also been deposited with the Ashmolean Museum.

RADIOCARBON DATES

All radiocarbon dates in this text are quoted as calibrated date ranges at two standard deviations (95.46% confidence). They have been calibrated with the calibration data provided by Stuiver *et al.* (1998), using OxCal (v3.5; Bronk Ramsey 1995; 1998). The date ranges have been calculated using the maximum intercept method (Stuiver and Reimer 1986), and are quoted in the form recommended by Mook (1986). Since the error terms are all greater than 25 radiocarbon years, the end points have been rounded out to the nearest 10 years.

PUBLICATION

This volume is a summary of a more detailed report (hereafter 'Detailed report') which can be downloaded as PDF files from the Oxford Archaeology website (http://thehumanjourney/springroad). The online report includes a more detailed introduction and site description (Chapters 1–2) and full versions of all of the specialists reports (Chapters 3–5), including their accompanying tables. The discussion (Chapter 6), however, is the same as that provided in this volume. All of the figures on the website are also reproduced in this volume with the same numbering.

Chapter 2:   Archaeological Description

by Zena Kamash and Tim Allen

NEOLITHIC AND BEAKER FEATURES (Fig. 4)

Grooved Ware pit 2622 in Area 8 (Fig. 5)

A single pit containing Grooved Ware (2622) was found in the south-western corner of Area 8. The pit was circular in plan, was 1.45 m wide and 0.55 m deep, with steeply sloping sides and a slightly concave base. There were four fills. The primary fill (2621) probably derived from natural erosion of the pit sides, and contained only a few finds. The dark colour of the two major fills of this pit (2620 and 2619), as well as the high density and character of the finds from them, suggests that they were deliberately deposited. The uppermost fill (2623) contained very few finds, and may have resulted from natural erosion of the surrounding subsoil.

Beaker Burial 3037 in Area 5 (Figs 6 and 22)

A single Beaker burial was found in Area 5 (Fig. 22). The subrectangular grave (3037), 1.6 m by 0.96 m wide and 0.14 m deep, had gently sloping sides and a flat base. Its shallow depth may be due to the compact nature of the periglacial clay within the gravel (3002) through which the grave was cut.

Although the grave was very shallow, it contained the intact skeleton of a 20–24 year old female (3036), oriented south-east (head) – north-west (feet), and crouched with the legs flexed and the head resting to the right. A copper awl (Fig. 6, SF 4) was positioned alongside the upper legs. A radiocarbon date of 2460–2200 cal BC was obtained from the skeleton.

Possible Beaker pit or posthole 2644 in Area 8

A circular posthole or pit (2644), 0.47 m wide and 0.33 m deep, was found on the western side of Area 8. It had near vertical sides and a flat base. It contained a very weathered, and hence probably residual Beaker sherd (Fig. 29, 8).

Other possible Neolithic features (Fig. 4)

Posthole 2122, in the central western part of Area 8, may be of Neolithic date. It was circular, 0.35 m wide and 0.13 m deep, with gently sloping sides and a concave base. It contained 18 pieces of Neolithic struck flint. The density and number of flints suggest that the material was not residual. However, the posthole cut an unexcavated soil mark which might have been a tree-throw hole from which the flint may have derived.

Modern grave 3506 (4 D 26) also contained a notable concentration (27 pieces) of Neolithic worked flint.

A well-preserved Peterborough Ware dish (Fig. 28) was recovered during modern grave-digging. Unfortunately its provenance was not recorded.

BRONZE AGE FEATURES (Fig. 4)

Timber circle 2568 and 2726 in Area 8 (Fig. 7; Pl. 2)

At the north end of Area 8 a double arc of postholes (Plate 2), probably part of a timber circle, was exposed. The surviving postholes formed an arc making up 60–80° of a circle. The diameter of the circle would have been around 18–20 m.

The posthole arc was sealed by a layer of dark brownish-red silty loam and gravel (2648) that was cut both by Saxon features and by posthole 2016 which contained five sherds (154 g) of middle Iron Age pottery. This sealing layer, which was up to 0.10 m deep, contained a significant proportion of gravel and may have been a ploughsoil.

Outer arc 2568

Because of their spatial arrangement, their common characteristics, and because many of them were overlain by layer 2648, 17 postholes have been assigned to the outer arc (group 2568) of the timber circle.

With one exception (2360) the postholes were large: 0.36–0.52 m wide and 0.45–0.66 m deep. The one smaller posthole (2360: 0.20 m wide and 0.41 m deep) was cut by a more substantial posthole (2357) and may have predated the circle. The postholes were either circular or oval in plan, and generally had flattish bases. Where they were oval, the long axis of the oval was generally aligned radially.

Post pipes were recognised in five postholes. The post pipes were all filled with friable mid to dark brownish-red clay silt, and the post packing was redeposited natural gravel and subsoil. The post pipes were invariably on the inner side of the arc, and the sections suggest that some of the post-pipes were only clipped when the postholes were half-sectioned. The section drawings do not, therefore, give an accurate indication of the original size of the post.

One of the oval postholes (2357) had a vertical inner side and a sloping outer side which may have been dug to assist in sliding the post in before standing it upright. The oval shape might, however, also have been formed if the post had been rocked to remove it. The sides of postholes 2094, 2090 and 2024 were irregular and widened on one or both sides towards the base (Fig. 7), possibly as a result of rocking. However, some of the postholes containing post pipes also had irregular sides.

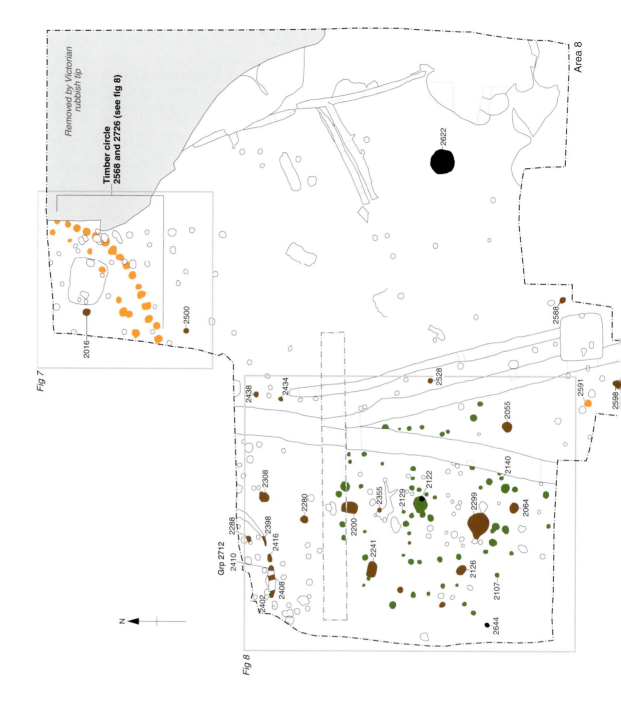

Figure 4 *Areas 8 and 9: Neolithic to Iron Age phases.*

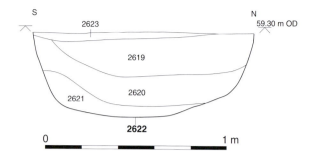

Figure 5   Section of Grooved Ware pit 2619.

The postholes were closely and fairly evenly spaced, the gaps between them being never less than 0.2 m and never more than 0.4 m. The gap between any two posts above ground is unlikely to have been more than 0.5 m, and most could have been arranged within the postholes to give an even spacing of 0.3–0.4 m.

Inner arc 2726

Seven postholes, spaced at *c* 1 m intervals (except *c* 2 m between 2328 and 2473), might have formed an inner arc. All of these postholes were circular except 2096, and varied in diameter from 0.23 m to 0.43 m and in depth from 0.08 m to 0.34 m. Most had steep sides, a concave base and a single fill of mid to dark greyish or reddish-brown sandy or clayey silt. Only posthole 2325 had a post pipe (2326), filled with a

friable mid brownish-red sandy silt, 0.15 m wide and 0.3 m deep, and surrounded by a friable mid yellowish-red sandy silt deposit (2327). Posthole 2096 (0.8 m by 0.4 m wide and 0.3 m deep) was subrectangular with an irregular base, and may have been a double posthole. It contained two fills, a friable greyish-red sandy silt (2097) overlain by a thin layer of friable dark greyish-brown clayey silt (2322).

Whether this group of postholes did form an arc is uncertain. The distribution of the postholes was not as regular as those in the outer arc, and none of them was sealed by layer 2648. Furthermore, two of them (2473 and 2032) might have been associated with a Saxon sunken-featured building (2008). These two postholes were not markedly different from the others in the circle, but the fill of posthole 2473 was very similar to the fills of the other internal Saxon postholes. Nevertheless, what dating evidence there is, is consistent with that from the outer arc.

Dating

Three of the postholes contained Neolithic pottery: a single, abraded sherd of early-middle Neolithic pottery came from the secondary fill (2091) of posthole 2090, a single sherd of Peterborough Ware (Fig. 29, 2) from the secondary fill (2093) of posthole 2092, and a single sherd of Grooved Ware (Fig. 29, 3) from the primary fill (2368) of posthole 2367. Radiocarbon dates on animal bone from the primary fill (2329) of posthole 2328 in the inner arc, and from the post

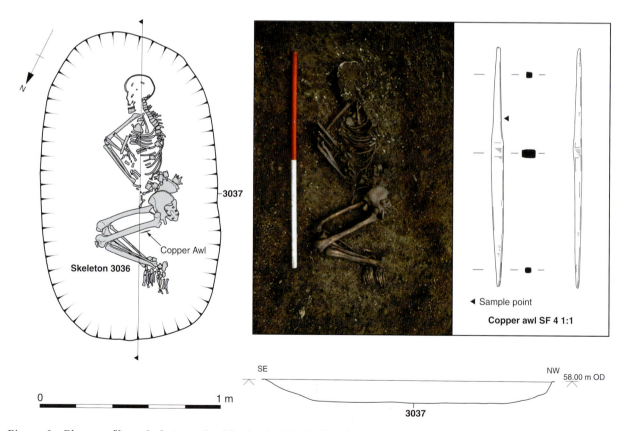

Figure 6   Plan, profile and photograph of Beaker burial 3037 and copper awl.

Plate 2 Timber circle and Sunken-featured Building 2008, taken from the south-west.

pipe (2375) of posthole 2373 in the outer arc produced dates of 1690–1510 cal BC and 1520–1310 cal BC respectively. The animal bones were sizeable and although one, which had been worked into a gouge or hide scraper, had been gnawed, were otherwise unabraded. Although the dates are not statistically consistent, they may bracket the period of use of the monument, as the earlier date came from a bone within the packing of a posthole, while the later date came from a bone within the fill of a post pipe, and so presumably post-dates the abandonment of the monument. A single, very small sherd of Iron Age pottery was found in the post pipe (2630) of posthole 2629. It is conceivable that the bones, like the Neolithic pottery, were residual, but on balance it seems more likely that the Iron Age potsherd was intrusive.

Pit 1201 in Area 9 (Fig. 4)

An oval pit (1201), 0.6 m long, 0.55 m wide, and 0.12 m deep, with gently sloping sides and a concave base, was found in the centre of Area 9 where it was cut by a Roman ditch (1629). The pit contained the base and lower sides of a large vessel that sat upright within, and almost filled, the pit (Plate 6).

Ditch groups 1199, 1206 and 1210 (Fig. 4)

Small quantities of Bronze Age pottery were found in two east-west ditches near the southern edge of Area 9: a large sherd from a Deverel-Rimbury Bucket Urn in ditch 1206 and four middle-late Bronze Age sherds in ditch 1199. Ditch 1199 also contained a burin, a side- and endscraper and a flake, and ditch 1206, seven flint flakes and a retouched flake. Despite solely Bronze Age finds, the spatial relationship of 1199 and 1206 to Roman ditches 1626 and 251 at right angles (see Fig. 14) suggests a Roman date. Ditch 1206 cut an undated ditch (1210) which may have been prehistoric.

Postholes in Areas 8 and 9 (Fig. 4)

Bronze Age pottery was found in a small number of further postholes: a small early-middle Bronze Age sherd in a posthole (2133) in Area 9; small numbers of middle-late Bronze Age sherds in six postholes in Area 9 and the southern part of Area 8, and a small late Bronze Age sherd in posthole 1442 in Area 9. The postholes do not form any coherent structures, the only indication of a focus of activity being four postholes (1329, 1442, 1298 and 1224) near the middle of Area 9.

Bronze Age finds from modern graves (Fig. 3)

Seven modern graves contained Bronze Age pottery: middle-late Bronze Age pottery in grave 3502 (plot 4 A 3) (5 sherds), grave 3514 (6 sherds) and grave 3501 (1 sherd); late Bronze Age pottery in grave 3522 (1 sherd), grave 3521 (1 sherd) and grave 3516 (a nearly complete bowl). Grave 3508 contained two late Bronze Age sherds and one middle-late Bronze Age sherd.

IRON AGE FEATURES

Iron Age roundhouse (Figs 8 and 9)

On the western edge of Area 8 an Iron Age roundhouse was identified, the eastern side of which had been partly destroyed by Roman ditches. Several slightly different posthole circuits are evident, not all of which need have been contemporary. The postholes have therefore been divided into the groups described below according to their possible relationships with the structure (Fig. 9). They consist of a symmetrically arranged post ring and porch (2719), inner (2724) and outer (2725) rings, internal partitions (2720 and 2721) and other central features (2723). A second phase of the roundhouse may be represented by a further ring of posts (2722). (The posthole dimensions and fills are tabulated in

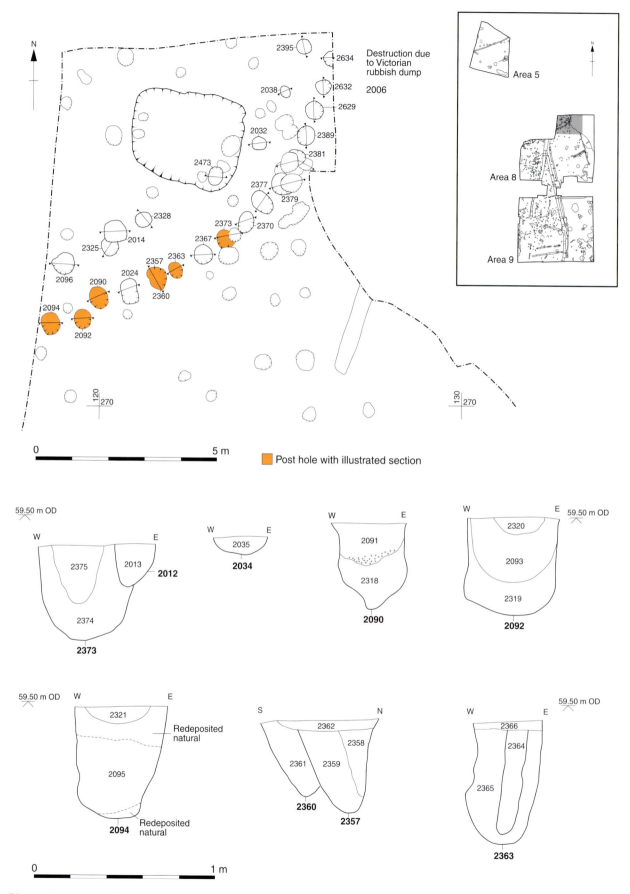

Figure 7 *Area 8: Plan of Bronze Age timber circle 2568 and sections of postholes.*

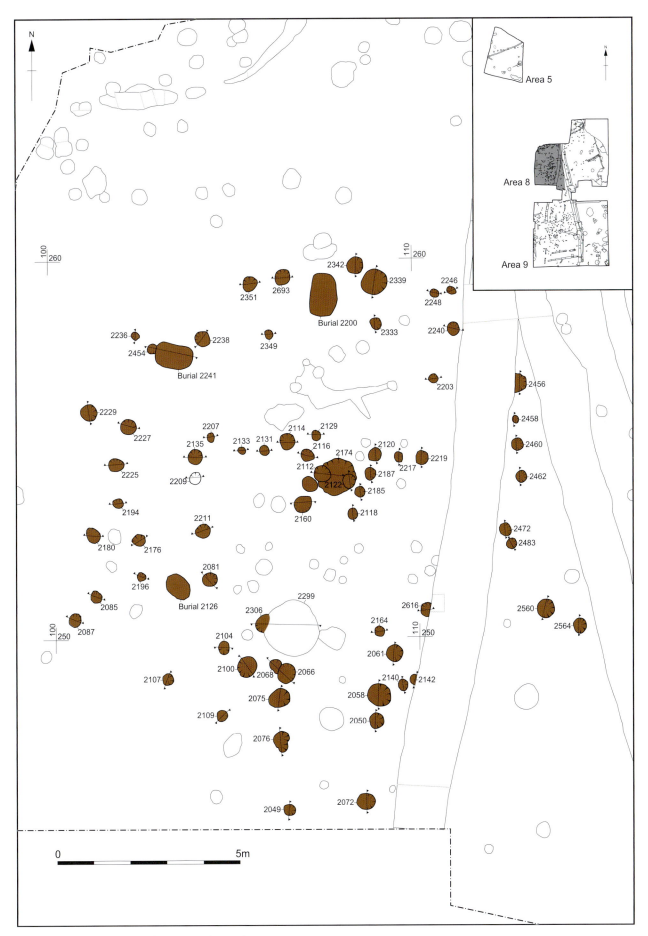

Figure 8   Area 8: Plan of Iron Age house in.

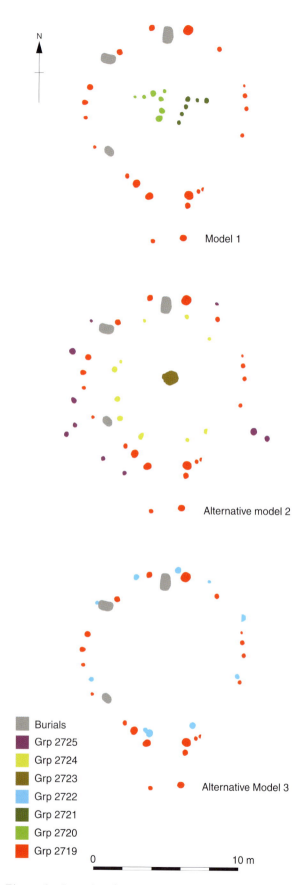

N

Model 1

Alternative model 2

Burials
Grp 2725
Grp 2724
Grp 2723
Grp 2722
Grp 2721
Grp 2720
Grp 2719

Alternative Model 3

0   10 m

Figure 9 Iron Age house: Some possible models for its structural development.

Appendix 1 in the Detailed Report available online; only the cut numbers are referred to in the text.)

Perhaps the clearest group (2719) consists of 21 postholes distributed symmetrically about a north-south axis. They define a ring and porch with the entrance facing south. The postholes defining the doorway were large compared to most of the others in the post ring.

The finds from this group consist of a small number of early and early-middle Iron Age sherds in 2140 and 2100, an unusual, probably late Bronze Age rim in posthole 2227, three fragments of unidentified animal bone in postholes 2339, 2227 and 2100, and a residual flint flake in posthole 2339.

Another ring of ten postholes (2722), slighly to the west of post ring 2719, may have been related to a preceding or succeeding structure with its entrance perhaps in almost the same location. The only finds from this group of features were 14 sherds of early-middle Iron Age pottery and five fragments of animal bone (including two of sheep mandible and one of sheep maxilla) in posthole 2061. Posthole 2066 contained a residual Neolithic levallois core.

Within the house, ten further postholes may have defined an inner post ring (2724). However, the distribution of the posts in this ring was rather irregular, and the postholes varied considerably in size. Only posthole 2306 contained any finds: seven sherds of early Iron Age pottery. Another (2616) was cut by a Roman ditch (2709). Some of the postholes may have belonged to later fences (Fig. 14, 2715 and 2717).

A further ten postholes may have defined an outer ring of posts (2725). Again, however, they varied considerably in size and shape, and their distribution was rather irregular. The only finds were two early Iron Age sherds in posthole 2107 and two late Bronze Age sherds in posthole 2180.

Near the centre of the roundhouse were two groups of postholes (2720 and 2721) that may have formed two symmetrically placed L-shaped partitions. The only finds in these postholes were a sherd of early-middle Iron Age pottery in fill 2129 and a residual early-middle Bronze Age sherd in fill 2133. It is, however, possible that posthole (2219) belonged to a Roman fence (2717).

At the very centre of the roundhouse lay two further postholes (2723) cutting a possible solution hollow. One of these (2122) contained the Neolithic flint mentioned above, and is unlikely to be contemporary with the roundhouse.

Human Burials (Figs 8 and 10–12)

Three burials were found in the area of the roundhouse. Radiocarbon determinations on samples of human bone suggest they date from the 4th–3rd century cal BC.

Grave 2126 (Fig. 10)

Grave 2126 was subcircular with a rounded base and steeply sloping sides at the south-eastern (head) end,

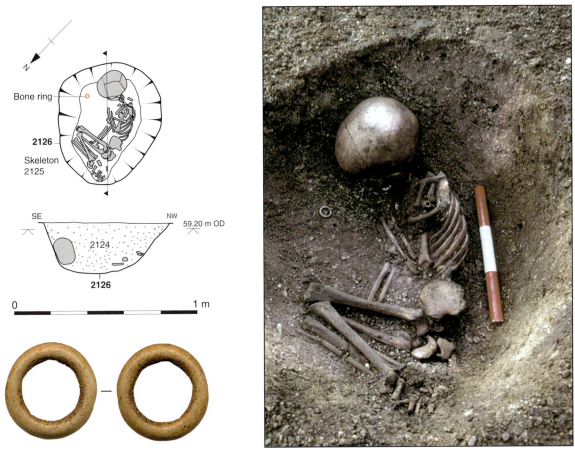

Figure 10   Plan, section and photograph of grave with child burial 2126 and bone ring.

becoming more gentle towards the north-western (foot) end. It was 0.68 m long, 0.55 m wide and 0.27 m deep (Fig. 11), and contained the skeleton (2125) of a four-five year old child (complete except for the upper right arm) as well as some bones from a three month-old infant. The child's body was crouched with the legs bent back under the patella, and the head to the right. A bone ring (Fig. 10, SF 5) was found near the skull. The grave also contained six sherds of residual early Iron Age pottery and some burnt limestone.

Grave 2241 *(Fig. 11)*

Grave 2241 was roughly subrectangular. It was 1.09 m long, 0.51 m wide and 0.20 m deep, and had a flat base with a steeply sloping edge on the south-eastern (foot) end which became more gentle towards the north-western (head) end. At the head end, a circular feature 2454, 0.21 m wide and 0.13 m deep with gently sloping sides and a concave base, had been cut. The grave contained the skeleton (2243) of a 19–21 year old male, the skull (except one fragment of occipital), mandible and some neck vertebrae were missing. The body was interred in a prone position (possibly pushed forwards into the pit) with

the upper legs brought up towards the chest and the lower legs flexed beneath them. The grave pit appeared to be too small for the burial, and feature 2454 may have been dug to accommodate the head. Alternatively feature 2454 might have been a later posthole that had removed the skull. No grave goods were found, but the grave contained seven residual early Iron Age sherds and some burnt limestone.

Grave 2200 *(Fig. 12)*

Grave 2200 was also subrectangular. It was 1.10 m long, 0.70 m wide, and 0.48 m deep, with a slightly irregular base and steeply sloping northern and southern sides. The eastern edge had a more gentle slope and the western edge was undercut, possibly to accommodate the right humerus and radius of the skeleton. The grave contained a nearly complete skeleton (2199) of a 20–24 year old man. The body was oriented north-south within the grave and was supine, with the back lying against the northern edge of the grave and the knees raised in a half-sitting position. A fragmentary spindle whorl and 21 residual sherds of early Iron Age pottery were retrieved from the uppermost fill of the grave, but may not have been deliberately incorporated into the grave.

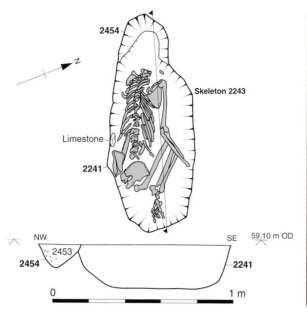

Figure 11   Plan, profile and photograph of grave with male burial 2241.

Other possible burials (Fig. 3)

A further burial possibly of Iron Age date was distur-bed by gravediggers in modern grave 3503 (4 A 4). This burial was crouched, laid on its left side and facing west. The skull was missing. Two sherds of early Iron Age pottery were recovered from the fill, as well as one sherd of 2nd-century AD pottery; this last may have come from the ploughsoil or topsoil overlying the grave.

In 1999 grave diggers found a crouched inhuma-tion which might have been of similar date in the north-western area of the cemetery. OAU made a brief record of the burial, but there were no directly associated finds and no bone was retained for dating.

Pits (Figs 4, 8 and 13)

Four probably early Iron Age pits were found scat-tered across the site: 2299 (within the roundhouse)

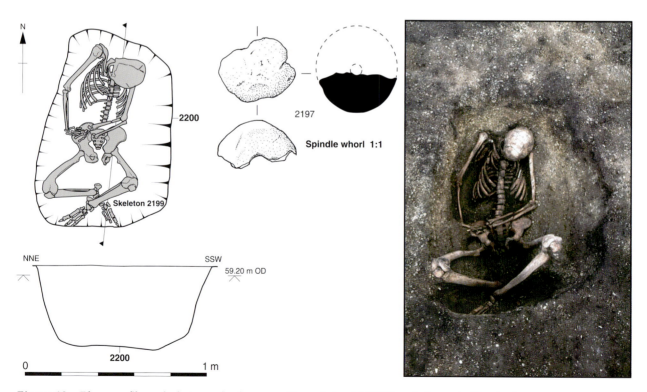

Figure 12   Plan, profile and photograph of grave with male burial 2200 and clay spindle whorl.

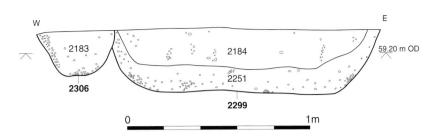

Figure 13   Section of Iron Age pit 2299 and posthole 2306.

and 2055 in Area 8, and 1207 and 605 in Area 9. Pits 2055 and 1207 were small, vertical-sided circular pits (0.6–0.78 m wide and 0.36–0.54 m deep), 2299 was large and shallow (1.64 m wide and 0.36 m deep; Fig. 13) and 605 was irregular (1.70 m wide and 0.96 m deep). They all contained Iron Age pottery as well as occasional residual earlier prehistoric sherds; pit 605 also contained one intrusive Roman sherd. The only other finds were a small quantity of animal bone and burnt limestone. Early Iron Age sherds were the only finds from pit 1008, but were probably residual.

Other postholes and curvilinear gully 2712 (Fig. 4)

A small number of probably Iron Age postholes were found scattered widely across the site, in no apparent pattern. These have been dated by the pottery they contained, but the possibility that the pot was residual cannot be excluded, especially in the case of posthole 2588, which may have belonged to a sunken-featured building (2687). Of these postholes, 13 have been dated to the early Iron Age, three to the early-middle Iron Age, and four to the middle Iron Age.

In the north-western corner of Area 8, one of the early-middle Iron Age postholes (2288) lay within a shallow, curvilinear segmented gully (2712; 0.10 m deep). This gully contained eight sherds of early-middle Iron Age pottery similar to that found in posthole 2288. The posthole might have formed part of structure contemporary with the gully. A further eight postholes were found within the area defined by the gully, but none contained any dateable artefacts, and since one was cut by the gully and another by posthole 2288, they cannot all have been contemporary. The evidence for a structure is thus slight.

Alongside the small quantities of pottery, the postholes contained small quantities of fired clay and burnt stone.

Iron Age finds from modern graves (Fig. 3)

Iron Age pottery has been found in several modern graves, mostly in small quantities (graves 3507 and 3518) but occasionally in larger groups (grave 3525: 27 sherds of early and early-middle Iron Age pottery). More mixed assemblages, containing late Bronze-early Iron Age (grave 3515) and Saxon (graves 3521 and 3516) pottery, as well as large quantities of Iron Age pottery, have also been found. The largest

proportion of early Iron Age pottery came from Area 11.

ROMAN FEATURES (Fig. 14)

Roman enclosure ditches belonging to two phases were found. Ditches of the first phase, dating from the 2nd century AD, were generally aligned NNW-SSE (although the largest ditch runs almost N-S at its southern end). Ditches of the second phase, dating to the late 2nd-3rd century AD, were aligned NNE-SSW.

One of the later ditches (1627) cut a posthole alignment on the same line (1631). A number of other possible posthole alignments were identified either parallel to, or at right angles to, these ditches, and may have been further Roman boundaries (see Figs 14–16). It must be stressed, however, that there is almost no dating evidence to link these postholes to one another, or to the Roman period. (The details of these postholes are given in Appendix 1 of the Detailed Report available online.)

Central ditch complex and fences in the 2nd century AD (Figs 15–17; Pl. 3)

The earlier Roman system consisted of four parallel sets of ditches and possible fence lines running NNW-SSE, 10–25 m apart, between which further ditches and fencelines ran at right-angles, at similar intervals, forming small rectangular enclosures.

The NNW-SSE aligned features consist of two parallel ditches (2710=1626 and 2711=1628) (Fig. 17, section A) running through the centre of both Areas 8 and 9, a short stretch of fence (1637) alongside 1626, two shallow ditches 2584 (Fig. 17, section F) and 2583 forming a single boundary in the north-east corner of Area 8 (with a return 2586 and a parallel ditch 2585 at right angles – Fig. 17, section G), two parallel ditches and a fence line (619, 615 and 1630) in the south-west corner of Area 8, and a possible short length of fence (2715) near the western edge of Area 8.

Both the central NNW-SSE aligned ditches and ditch 2584 terminated in line with one another just short of the northern edge of Area 8, where the end of 2710 was cut away by a ditch (2709) belonging to the later system. Just to the north of the end of these ditches, a possible long fence line (2713) ran at right angles to them much of the way across Area 8. To the south of this, a number of other fences and ditches

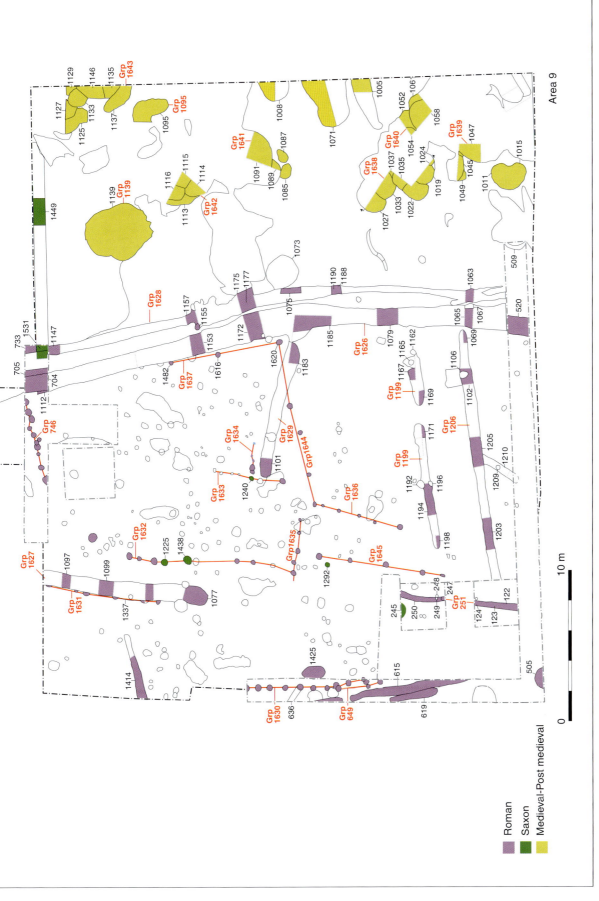

Figure 14 *Areas 8 and 9: Roman, Saxon, medieval and post-medieval phases.*

Roman

Saxon

Medieval-Post medieval

Area 9

10 m

0

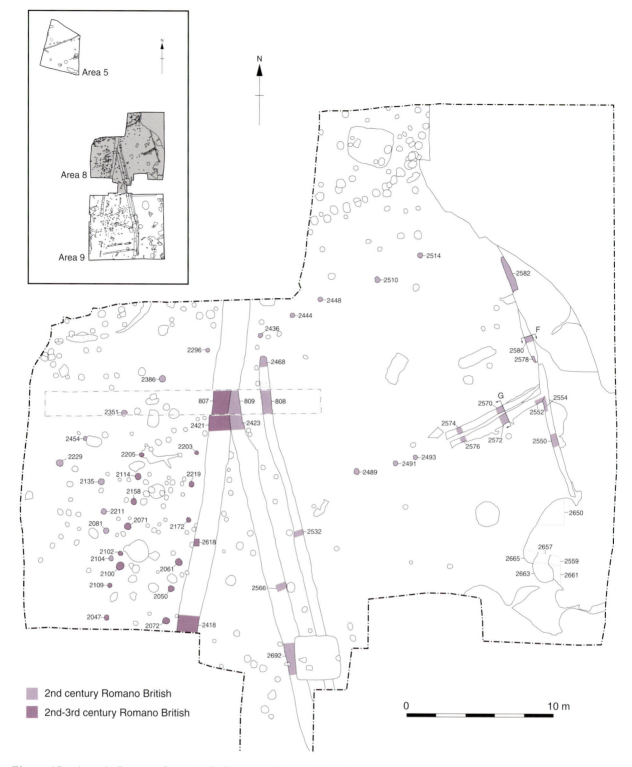

Figure 15 Area 8: Roman phases including possible posthole alignments.

ran on the same alignment: ditches 2585 and 2586 – which may have continued as fence 2714 – in Area 8; fence 746 at the northern edge of Area 9; ditch 1414 at the western edge of Area 9; fence 1644 starting from the south end of fence 1637, and ditches 1199 (Fig. 17, sections C & D) and 1206 (Fig. 17, section E) near the southern edge of Area 9.

The largest of the ditches in this group was 2710=1626, which was up to 1.80 m wide and 0.55 m deep (Fig. 17, sections A & B). Most of the other ditches were smaller, measuring 0.20 m–0.85 m wide and 0.04–0.22 m deep.

Most of these features contained few finds. However, large quantities of 2nd century pottery were

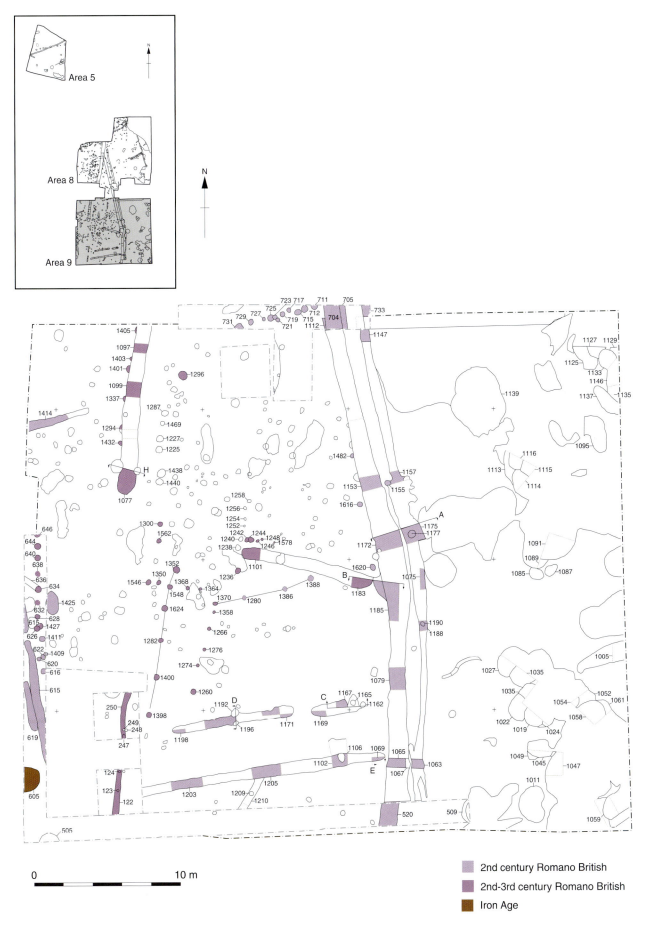

Figure 16   Area 9: Roman phases including possible posthole alignments.

2nd century Romano British

2nd-3rd century Romano British

Iron Age

0   10 m

found in ditch 2710=1626, including some in its primary fill. Similar pottery was found in ditch 1414 (Fig. 16), and Roman ceramic building material was found in ditch 2586. The remaining features have been dated on the basis of their alignments. A small number of residual, earlier finds, including a Deverel-Rimbury sherd in ditch 1206 and middle-late Bronze Age pottery in ditches 2710=1626 and 1199 were also found. Later material was also recovered, including probably intrusive 3rd–4th-century pottery and a very fresh-looking 4th-century coin in the secondary fills of ditch 2710=1626, and clay pipe and early medieval pottery in a disturbed section (1112) of the same ditch.

Central ditch complex in the late 2nd–early 3rd century (Figs 14–17; Pl. 3)

Towards the end of the 2nd century, new ditches (2709 and 1627), up to 1.25 m wide and 0.43 m deep (Fig. 17, section H, ditch 1627), were dug running NNE, 2709 cutting the end of one of the earlier ditches (2710). Although on the same alignment, these two later ditches (2709 and 1627) do not line up, and so presumably ended in the baulk between Areas 8 and 9. Ditch 1627 contained much 2nd- and 3rd-century pottery, especially at the southern end (Fig. 32); ditch 2709 later 2nd-century pottery. A smaller ditch (251; 0.30 m wide), running from the southern edge of Area 9, forms a continuation of the same line. A short length of ditch (1629) (0.75 m wide and 0.20 m deep) (Fig. 17, section B) was dug at right angles to 1627 from the western edge of earlier ditch 1626, and was aligned just south of the end of 1627. Ditch 1629 also contained a sizeable assemblage of 2nd-century

pottery. The fact that ditch 2709 cut across the very end of 2710, and that 1629 was dug westwards from it, suggests that the earlier ditches were still visible, so that the new ditches would have formed a triangular enclosure with its entrance to the south.

Ditch 1627 cut a line of postholes (1631) on its western edge; ditch 2709 may also have had a fence (2717) alongside (Fig. 14). A second possible fence (2716) ran parallel to ditch 2709, 4 m to the west. Further possible fences on this alignment were found to the east of ditches 1627 and 251 (1632, 1633, 1636 and 1645), and another (1635) lay at right angles (Pl. 3). One 2nd century sherd came from the posthole lines; otherwise finds were of Bronze Age and Iron Age pottery. Four postholes (1292, 1225, 1438 and 1240) in fences 1632, 1633 1645 and contained small Anglo-Saxon sherds, and it is possible that some of these fence lines were post-Roman.

Pits in Area 9 (Fig. 16)

Two pits containing small quantities of 2nd-century pottery were found in Area 9, pit 1425 near the western edge and pit 505 in the south-west corner. Both were oval with gently sloping sides and flat or uneven bases (1.3–1.5 m wide and 0.24–0.7 m deep). One Roman pottery sherd, believed to be intrusive, was found in a nearby Iron Age pit (605).

Modern graves 3509 and 3531 (Fig. 3)

Roman pottery has been found in two recent graves: three sherds of 2nd-century pot with one early-middle Iron Age sherd and one 11th-century sherd in grave 3509, and 54 Roman sherds in grave 3531.

Plate 3   General view of excavation with Area 9 in the foreground, looking north-west.

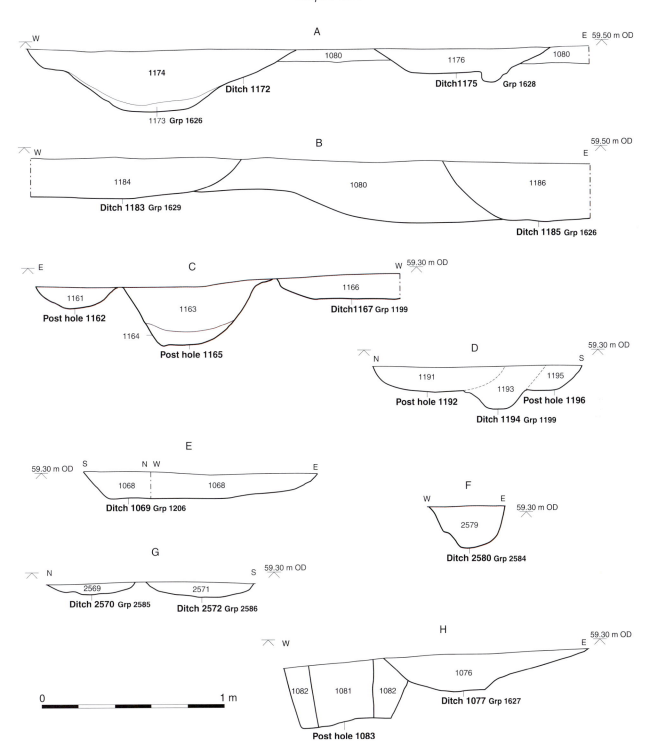

Figure 17   Sections of Roman ditches.

SAXON FEATURES

Sunken-featured buildings in Area 8 (Figs. 14 and 18–19; Pls 2 and 4)

Two sunken-featured buildings (SFBs) were found in Area 8, one (2008) near the northern edge, the other (2687) near the southern, where it cut a Roman ditch (2710). Both were subrectangular features, similar in size (2008: 3.05 m by 2.26 m wide and 0.28 m deep; 2687: 3.12 m by 2.90 m and 0.26 m deep).

Postholes were found within both SFBs at the eastern and western ends: one at each end (2706 and 2702) of SFB 2687 (Fig. 18; Pl. 4) but two (2624 and 2626) at the west and one deep example (2477) at the east in SFB 2008 (Fig. 19; Pl. 2). Further postholes were also found within both: two (2473 and 2475) in the south-east corner of SFB 2008 and one (2698) in the south-west corner of SFB 2687. However, post-hole 2473 may have been part of the Bronze Age timber circle and thus unrelated to the SFB. All of

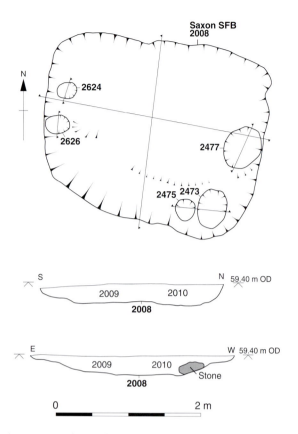

Figure 18 Plan and sections of Sunken-featured Building 2008.

the internal postholes were covered by the fills of the SFBs. Posthole 2690 in SFB 2687 was partially covered by a limestone slab, one of two such slabs found within this SFB.

Further postholes were also found around both of the SFBs (Fig. 14). There were six around SFB 2008, although one of them (2032) may have belonged to the timber circle, and another contained five middle Iron Age sherds. The six postholes around SFB 2687 might have been related to a structure, postholes 2683 and 2595 forming the north-western and south-western corners, between which lay posthole 2685. Posthole 2540 lay on the northern side, and postholes 2588 and 2704 near the north-eastern corner. However, posthole 2588 contained two sherds of early Iron Age pottery, and may date from that phase.

SFB 2687 had three fills. The primary fill (2686) contained just 15 sherds of undecorated early Saxon pottery, but the secondary fill (2673) contained 79 Saxon sherds including some that were stamped and incised, and the upper fill (2672) contained 147 early Saxon sherds as well as large quantities of articulated animal bone. SFB 2008 had only a single fill, which contained 55 sherds of undecorated Anglo-Saxon pottery, daub, an iron nail and animal bone.

Pits and postholes (Fig. 14)

Saxon pottery was also found in a posthole (2209) in Area 8, in a pit or quarry (1449) south-east of SFB 2687, in four postholes (1292, 1225, 1438 and 1240) in the SW of Area 9, and in a pit (245) in the same area. The postholes in Area 9 were all attributed to fences (1225 and 1438 to fence 1632, 1292 to fence 1645, and 1240 to fence 1633), and it is possible that these alignments were not Roman but Saxon. A number of posthole lines at right angles are evident, but no convincing buildings could be found. Pit (245)

Plate 4 Saxon Sunken-featured Building 2687 completely excavated, looking east.

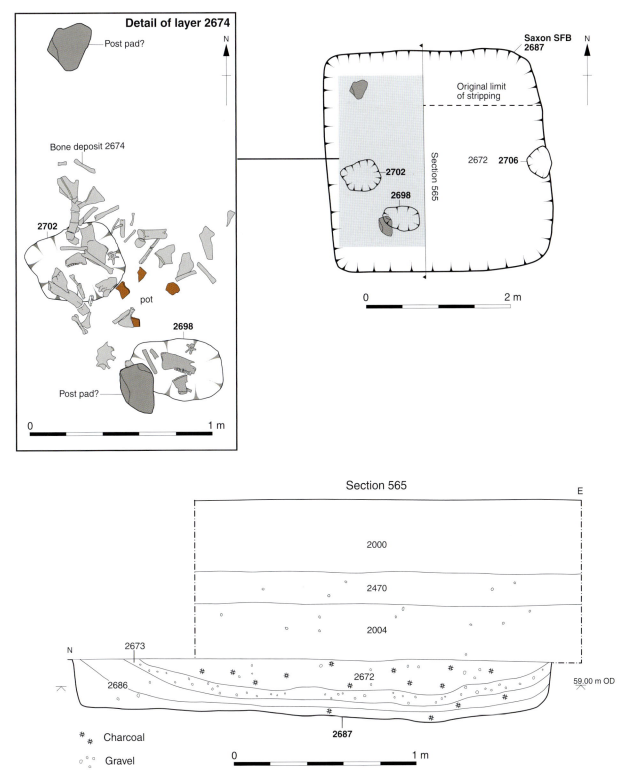

Detail of layer 2674

Post pad?

N

Bone deposit 2674

2702

pot

2698

Post pad?

0   1 m

Saxon SFB 2687

N

Original limit of stripping

Section 565

2672   **2706**

2702

2698

0   2 m

Section 565

E

2000

2470

2004

2673

2686

2672

2687

59.00 m OD

Charcoal

o   Gravel

0   1 m

Figure 19   Plans and section of Sunken-featured Building 2687 with detail of bone deposit.

contained a perforated Roman coin and a perforated Roman brooch as well as early-middle Saxon pottery. Feature 1449 contained a wide variety of finds – bone, glass, flint and Saxon pottery – and is probably a medieval quarry that had disturbed a Saxon feature.

Saxon archaeology and modern graves (Figs 3 and 20)

Saxon pottery has been found in numerous modern graves. The largest concentration, consisting of 103 grass-tempered sherds (Berisford 1973, fig. 39, 6–8), came from one or more large features cut by a group of

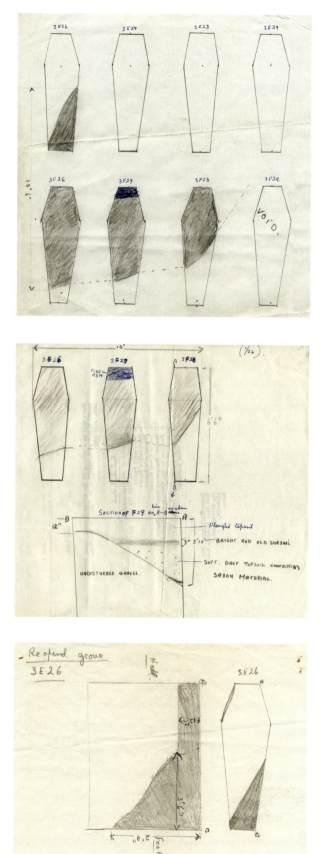

Figure 20 Gravedigger plans and section of Saxon features found in modern graves.

four graves (Figs 3 and 21, 3526 (3 E 26), 3527 (3 F 26), 3528 (3 F 27), and 3529 (3 F 28)). It is possible that modern graves have also disturbed Saxon burials. Case (1957) records the extended burial of a young adult which was partially overlain by a further skeleton. The skulls of both lay to the north. Two further possibly Saxon burials, this time contracted, seem also to have been found, but were not recorded in detail.

MEDIEVAL AND POST-MEDIEVAL FEATURES

Medieval pits in Areas 8 and 9 (Figs 14 and 21; Pl. 5)

Several groups of intercutting pits were found running along the eastern side of Areas 8 and 9, east of the Roman ditch 2710=1628. In Area 8 the pits cut into Roman gully 2584. The pits were very varied in shape, profile and size (0.80–2.4 m wide and from 0.15–0.95 m deep). This variation suggests that they were dug for gravel-extraction. Gravel spills in some of these pits indicate that they were left open after the gravel was extracted, filling slowly thereafter. They contained a wide range of finds, usually in quite small quantities, and of varying dates. Some, eg Pit 1008 (Area 9), contained only prehistoric finds. The latest finds in a group sectioned in Area 8 were early-middle Saxon; in Area 9 middle-late Bronze Age, early-middle Iron Age, Roman, early-middle Saxon and 12th- to 13th-century pottery was found. The majority of the pottery is believed to be residual from features through which the medieval pits were cut. The medieval pits have, therefore, been dated by the latest, and largest sherds of pottery they contained: 12th- to13th-century pottery in pits 1071, 1139 and 1146. All of the pits were overlain by the ploughsoils of late medieval date that covered the whole excavation area.

Posthole group 3034 (Fig. 22)

In Area 5, a line of eight postholes (seven large and one small) was found. Their stratigraphic position, and a fragment of clay pipe found in one of them suggest that they were post-medieval.

Victorian quarry 2006 (Fig. 14)

In the north-eastern corner of Area 8 a large Victorian quarry filled with domestic rubbish, including 19th-century ceramics and glass, was excavated by machine. It had obliterated any archaeology in this area of the site.

Layers and ploughsoils

Following the Saxon occupation there was a build-up of soil across the site. In general, the archaeology was sealed by a ploughsoil 0.4 m to 0.6 m deep that was directly overlain by the topsoil. This ploughsoil contained a wide range of residual Iron Age and Roman pottery as well as medieval, post-medieval and modern wares which suggest that it was cultivated in the medieval and post-medieval period.

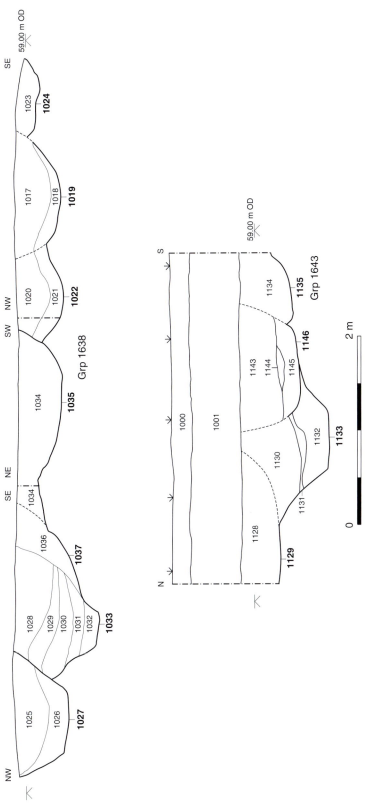

Figure 21   Sections of medieval gravel extraction pits.

Plate 5   Medieval gravel pits in Area 9, from the west.

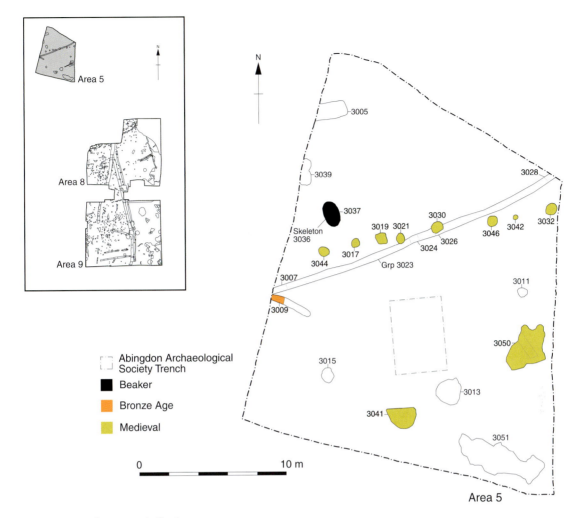

Figure 22   Area 5: features of all phases.

The post-medieval map evidence indicates that the site was used as agricultural land and allotments until it was converted into a cemetery.

Medieval finds in modern graves (Fig. 3)

A wire-wound pin, dating from the 13th century or later, was found near to the shoulder of an extended burial which was revealed in a modern grave cut by the hedge in Section 3 of the municipal cemetery. The burial was aligned south (head) – north (feet). The skull was missing.

The only other significant medieval finds in modern graves were twenty-six sherds of 13th century pottery found in modern grave 3513 (6 C 16).

31

Chapter 3:   The Finds

STRUCK FLINT (Figs 23–27)
Summary of report by Hugo Lamdin-Whymark

A total of 667 flints and 88 g of burnt unworked flint was recovered from the excavations and from recent grave digging. A third of all of the flint came from late Neolithic Grooved Ware pit 2622. Much of the rest of the flint, some of Mesolithic date, but mostly of mid-late Neolithic date, was residual. The collection of flint from recent graves seems to have been biased towards retouched flints and blades rather than flakes, and Bronze Age flint may be under-represented.

No flint occurs naturally in the gravels on which the site lies, and all of the flint has been imported – mid to dark grey flint perhaps from chalk outcrops to the south, brown flint perhaps from river gravels to the south-east, and Bullhead flint from an unknown source.

The Mesolithic flint consists of six narrow blades, a single platform bladelet core, a truncated blade, a burin, and an end scraper.

The mid-late Neolithic material includes flakes, mainly relatively thin broad flakes of mixed hammer mode (a similar technology to the group from pit 2622), a mixture of single and multi-platform flake cores, and a later Neolithic levallois core. The retouched flint includes three later Neolithic chisel arrowheads, five serrated flakes – two of which exhibit silica gloss – numerous scrapers, two backed knifes and two flakes from reworked polished implements.

Pit 2622

The Grooved Ware pit 2622 contained a total of 221 flints, mostly in the secondary deposits (2620 and 2619). The tertiary deposit (2623) contained only two flakes. The composition of the assemblages in layers 2620 and 2619 is very different: whereas fill 2620 contained a single core and seven retouched tools, fill 2619 contained two cores, a tested nodule and only a single retouched artefact.

The flint was in a very fresh, uncorticated condition; no post-depositional edge damage was noted, indicating that none of the flint was residual. A total of 74 flints were broken, and fifteen were burnt.

A number of deliberate breaks were noted, some perhaps for the creation of fragments for use, as some of these pieces were well used (although not along the snapped edges). The breaks could also have occurred after use. Deliberate non-functional breakage is also present: end scraper SF 44 (Fig. 27, 4) was deliberately struck into two pieces and only the distal fragment deposited in the pit. It is possible that the snapping relates to transverse arrowhead manufacture.

The pit contained a total of 8.6% blades, which falls within Ford's (1987, 79) 7–14% bracket for the proportion of blades in later Neolithic assemblages. The average size of the flint from the pit is relatively small at 25 mm long by 22 mm wide (Fig. 23).

The majority of the flints recovered are non-cortical flakes (Fig. 24, 1–4), perhaps indicating that the nodules were prepared away from the pit. The presence of three rejuvenation flakes, including a rejuvenation tablet, suggests that the cores were worked relatively carefully; platform edge abrasion on 41% of the flakes and the dominance of feather terminations also supports this suggestion.

The three cores recovered from the pit are the three heaviest from the site (bar a single unstratified example), suggesting that the cores in the pit may not have been exhausted before disposal.

A high proportion of flints (91) bore edge damage resulting from use. Whilst, however, the majority of flakes under 20 mM^2 have not been utilised, all of the flakes over 40 mM^2 in the pit have been utilised (Fig. 25), perhaps indicating that whilst a small proportion of knapping debris was present, the larger flints have all been utilised. The fact that use-wear was present on both the heavily worn artefacts and the majority of the fresh flints suggests that 'unused' or 'still functional' flakes were not deposited.

The use damage identified in the pits shows a broad range of actions and hardness of contact materials (Fig. 26, 1–6). Scraping forms a significant proportion

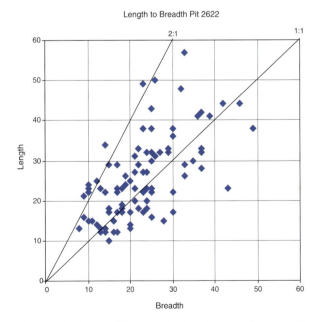

Figure 23   Struck flint: Graph showing length to breadth ratios of the struck flint from pit 2622.

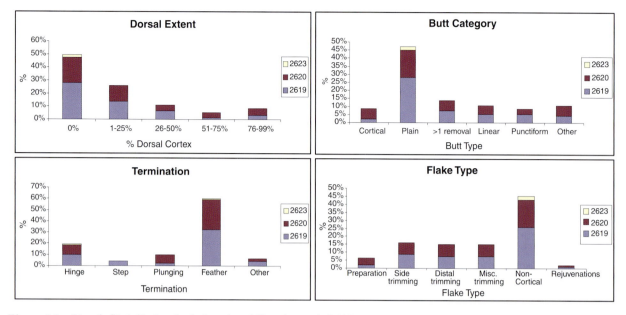

Figure 24   Struck flint: Technological traits of flint from pit 2622.

of the actions, and the presence of five rounded edges resulting from scraping possibly indicates flints associated with hide processing (Akoshima 1987, 76). However, cutting and whittling actions predominate, comparatively few of which were on soft materials, indicating that the cutting and whittling of flesh or fleshy plant materials represented a minimal element of the use-wear.

Silica gloss was located behind the teeth of a serrated flake. Silica gloss commonly occurs on the teeth of serrated flakes, where it accumulates as a result of the cutting and whittling of silica-rich plants (Juel Jensen 1994, 62–63; Unger-Hamilton 1988).

The flintwork recovered from Grooved Ware pit 2622 forms a relatively large, coherent assemblage, comparable to assemblages from Grooved Ware pits at Barrow Hills, Radley (Barclay 1999) and Cassington (Case 1982). The high proportion of utilised flints is comparable with that from the Peterborough Ware and Grooved Ware pits at Dorney in the Middle Thames Valley (Lamdin-Whymark forthcoming). The low proportions of soft cutting and whittling activities in pit 2622, and the higher frequency of hard cutting and whittling actions, is also comparable to that in the Peterborough and Grooved Ware associated assemblages at Dorney.

Catalogue of illustrated flints (Fig. 27)

Mesolithic

1 **Blade**, broken. Unstratified. OCMS 1994.34.
2 **Burin** manufactured transversely on a flake. Context 1193. Acc. No. 89.121.

Neolithic

Late Neolithic pit 2622

3 Distal fragment of a snapped **flake**. Snapped by a blow to the ventral surface. Note the fracturing present on the ventral surface. Context 2620. SF 30.
4 **End and side scraper**. Distal fragment, snapped by a blow to the dorsal surface. Context 2620. SF 44.
5 Medial fragment of a snapped **blade**. Context 2620. SF 103.
6 **Snapped flake**. Context 2619. SF 50.
7 Conjoining fragments of a snapped **flake**. Context 2619. SF 153 and SF 154.
8 **Multi-platform flake core**. Context 2619. SF 53.

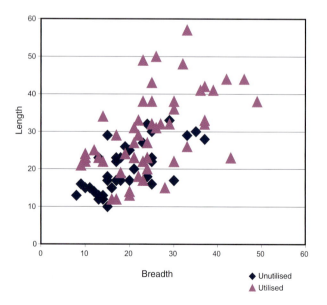

Figure 25   Struck flint: Graph plotting length to breadth ratio of flint flakes against the presence of use damage.

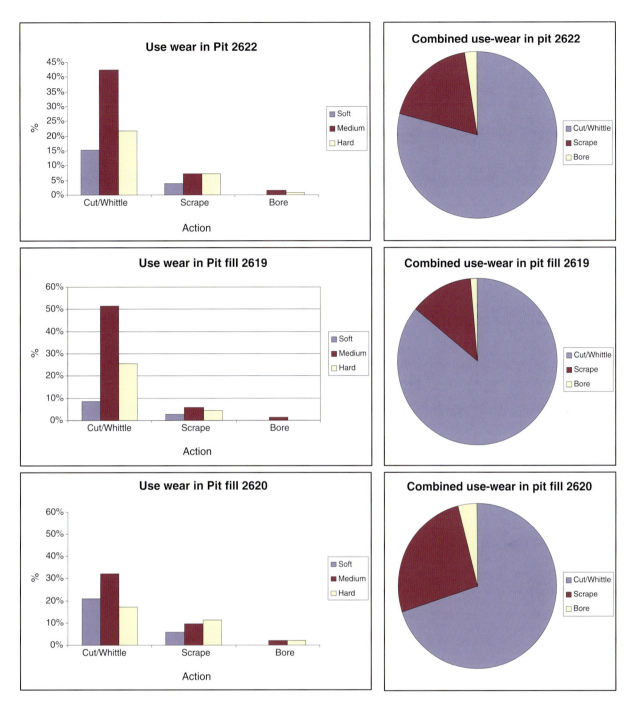

Figure 26   Struck flint: Use-wear evidence for flint from pit 2622, displayed by context and overall.

Other Neolithic flintwork

9   **Chisel arrowhead**. Context 3506, OCMS 1994.34.

10   Fragmentary **chisel arrowhead**. Unstratified. OCMS 1994.34.

11   **Chisel arrowhead**? Context 1134. Acc. No. 89.121.

12   **Levallois-style flake core**. Context 2065. Acc. No. 89.121.

13   **Backed knife**. Context 2123. Acc. No. 89.121.

STONE

Summary of report by Hugo Lamdin-Whymark

Numerous pieces of ironstone, quartzite, sandstone and limestone were recovered during the excavations. None showed any signs of use, but a piece of water-worn shelly limestone, from sunken-featured building 2008, might have been used as a working surface or as a structural element such as a post pad. Two belemnite fossils and one ammonite were

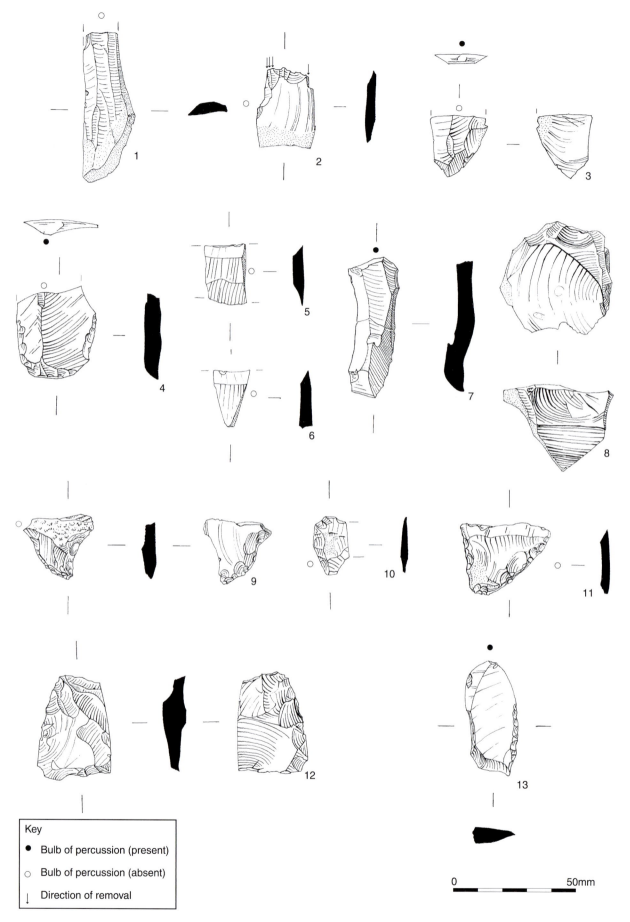

Key

● Bulb of percussion (present)

○ Bulb of percussion (absent)

↓ Direction of removal

0   50mm

Figure 27   Struck flint implements.

recovered from the same sunken-featured building. Although they occur locally they might have been collected.

NEOLITHIC AND EARLY BRONZE AGE POTTERY

Summary of report by Alistair Barclay

Although only a small assemblage of 36 sherds (372 g) of earlier prehistoric pottery was found during the excavation and as a result of recent grave digging, every major ceramic tradition, from the early Neolithic to the early Bronze Age is represented.

The fabrics (Table 1) are all typical of their periods, and could all have been made locally. The early and middle Neolithic Plain Bowl and Peterborough Ware traditions are flint tempered (although one grog tempered middle Neolithic fabric was identified), the late Neolithic Grooved Ware is grog and shell tempered, and the Beaker and early Bronze Age pottery is grog tempered.

Plain Bowl

Just five, small, abraded, plain, flint tempered sherds probably belonging to the Plain Bowl tradition were found. They were all residual. Plain Bowl pottery was probably in use from *c* 4100–3300 cal BC.

Peterborough Ware

Peterborough Ware is represented by just over half of an irregular elliptical mouthed dish with a rounded profile flattened at the base (Fig. 28, 1), and a single, very abraded residual sherd with cord impressed decoration (Fig. 29, 2). The context of the dish is unknown. Its entire surviving external surface was decorated with an incised herringbone pattern which extends also into the interior and onto the base. An impressed pattern of three possibly interlocked grooves on the base may be the result of the vessel being placed on a mat before it had dried.

Oval dishes in the Peterborough Ware tradition have been found in Wiltshire (Piggott 1962, fig. 13. P25; Cleal 1990, 30 and fig. 21 P273), Yorkshire (Manby 1995, fig. 55.1), Middlesex (Grimes 1960, fig 78, 20) and Oxfordshire (Barclay and Edwards in prep.) in association with both Mortlake and Fengate style vessels. The herringbone decoration and the rounded, flattened based profile perhaps relate the Spring Road dish to the Mortlake style. However, the grog tempered fabric is more typical of the Fengate style in the Upper Thames Valley. It probably dates from the late 4th to the early 3rd millennium cal BC. A sufficient number of shallow dishes have now been found to suggest that the early Neolithic ceramic set of bowl and cup was expanded in the

Table 1   Neolithic and early Bronze Age pottery fabrics.

Early Neolithic (Plain Bowl)	
Flint-tempered	
F2/EN	Hard fabric with sparse medium angular flint (1–3 mm)
F3/EN	Hard fabric with sparse medium to coarse angular flint (3 mm)
FA2/EN	Hard fabric with sparse medium angular flint (1–3 mm) and rare coarse quartz sand
Middle Neolithic (Peterborough Ware)	
Flint-tempered	
F2/MN	Hard fabric with sparse medium angular flint (1–3 mm)
Grog-tempered	
GAV2/MN	Hard fabric with moderate medium-size angular grog (1–3 mm), moderate rounded voids (?leached calcareous grit) and rare quartz sand
Late Neolithic (Grooved Ware)	
Grog-tempered	
G2/LN	Hard fabric with moderate medium angular grog (1–3 mm)
GF2/LN	Hard fabric with moderate medium angular grog (1–3 mm) and rare angular flint
Shell-tempered	
S2/LN	Hard fabric with common shell platelets (sometimes leached) (1–3 mm)
Late Neolithic/early Bronze Age (Beaker)	
Grog-tempered	
G2/LNEBA	Hard fabric with moderate angular grog
GA2/LNEBA	Hard micaceous fabric with moderate angular grog and common black, red and quartz sand
GAF2/LNEBA	Hard fabric with moderate angular grog, rare sand and rare flint
GF2/LNEBA	Hard fabric with moderate angular grog and rare flint
Early Bronze Age	
Grog-tempered	
G1/EBA	soft fabric with moderate small grog (1 mm)
GF2/EBA	soft fabric with moderate small to medium angular grog (up to 3 mm) and sparse flint (up to 3 mm). Fabric also contains rare flint gravel, quartz and organics (voids)

middle Neolithic to include a variety of shallow and deep oval dishes.

Grooved Ware

A small number of Grooved Ware sherds were found (Fig. 29, 3–5), 5 sherds in the Woodlands substyle in pit 2622 (Fig. 29, 4–5) and one rim from a plain vessel possibly in the Durrington Walls substyle (Fig. 29, 3)

in one of the postholes of the timber circle (Wainwright and Longworth 1971, 238–40, fig. 60 P478–89). The former include thin walled sherds, decorated with horizontal and oblique bands of plain and decorated raised cordons (Fig. 29, 4). Another sherd has finger-tipped decoration (Fig. 29, 5). Similar Durrington Walls style pottery has been found at Radley (Barclay and Halpin 1999, fig. 4.4 P9) and Yarnton (Barclay and Edwards in prep.), and comparable

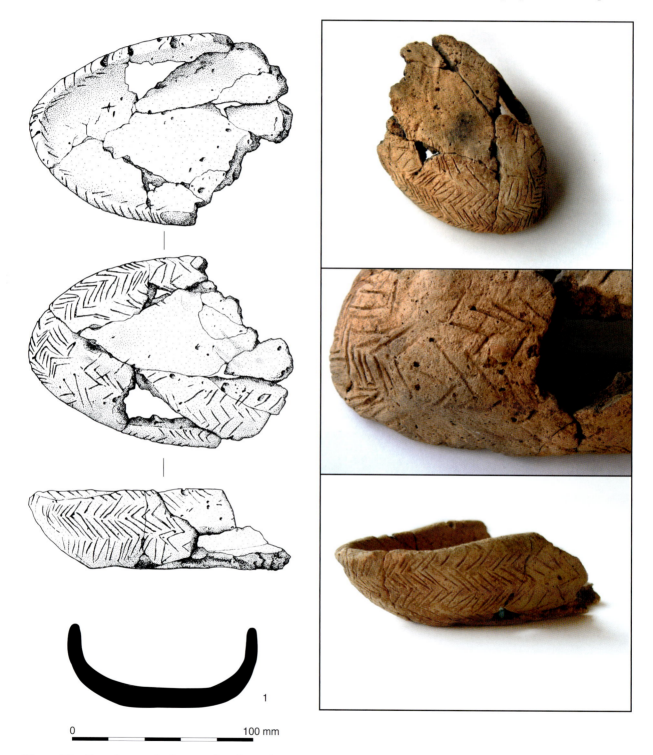

0   100 mm

Figure 28   Drawings and photographs of Peterborough Ware dish.

Woodlands style pottery has been found in pits at both Radley (Cleal 1999) and Sutton Courtenay (Leeds 1934).

Beaker

A total of five Beaker sherds, as well as seven plain sherds which could be late Neolithic or early Bronze Age, were found (Fig. 29, 6–8). All were residual, unstratified or in uncertain contexts. The Beaker sherds derived from at least three fineware vessels. The decoration consists of horizontal bands of comb impressions, a bounded cross-hatched motif and horizontal lines, which relate these sherds to Clarke's (1970) European and Wessex/Middle Rhine groups. These groups may be early in the Beaker period, *c* 2500–2000 cal BC (Needham 1996). Comparable vessels have been found, mostly in graves, at Radley (Cleal 1999), Drayton (Barclay *et al.* 2003) and Dorchester-on-Thames (Whittle *et al.* 1992). Similar pottery has, however, also been found on buried ground surfaces and in pits at Drayton (Cleal 2003) and Yarnton (Barclay and Edwards in prep.), and it seems that early Beaker finewares were used in both domestic and funerary contexts (Barclay and Edwards in prep; Barclay and Lupton 1999, 515).

Early Bronze Age

Just four sherds might date from the early Bronze Age. The grog tempered fabric is similar to a fabric used at Yarnton to make Biconical Urns. The pottery included base sherds with multiple perforations in the base and walls (Fig. 29, 9) which could be compared to early Bronze Age accessory vessels, although these have perforations in the walls only (Longworth 1983, fig. 23; Abercromby 1912, pl. LXXX, 239).

Illustrated catalogue (Figs 28–9)

1   **Peterborough Ware**. Mortlake/Fengate substyle. Middle Neolithic, Five conjoining sherds (158 g) make up just over half of an oval dish-shaped vessel. It has a rounded profile with a flattened base. Decorated all-over with a horizontal incised herringbone pattern, which spreads over the rim and also on to the base. The pattern on the sides runs in the same direction and converges near to the point of maximum rim diameter. The decoration is haphazard and asymmetrical with three and two rows of herringbone on different sides. Fabric GAV/MN. Colour: ext. yellowish-brown; core grey; int. yellowish-brown. Condition average. OCMS 1994.29. Unstratified.

2   **Peterborough Ware**, Middle Neolithic, Decorated body sherd (6 g) with horizontal bands of impressed whipped cord maggot. Fabric F2/MN. Colour: black throughout. Condition very worn. Context 2093.

3   **Grooved Ware**, ?Durrington Walls substyle, Late Neolithic. Simple pointed rim (5 g). Fabric GF2/LN. Colour: ext. yellowish-brown;

core & int. black. Condition average to worn. Context 2368.

4   **Grooved Ware**, Woodlands substyle, Late Neolithic,. Rim and body sherds (10 g) decorated with applied cordons. Fabric S2/LN. Colour: ext. greyish-brown; core black; int. greyish-black. Condition average to worn. Black carbonaceous residue below rim. Context 2620.

5   **Grooved Ware**, ?Woodlands substyle, Late Neolithic. Finger-tip impressed body sherd. Fabric S3/LN. Colour: ext. reddish-brown; core & int. grey. Condition average to worn. Context 2620.

6   **Beaker**, Late Neolithic/early Bronze Age. Rim and neck sherds with banded comb decoration. Fabric GAF2/LNEBA. Colour: ext. reddish-brown; black core; int. reddish-brown. Condition average. Ashmolean Museum 1972.21. Unstratified.

7   **Beaker**, Late Neolithic/early Bronze Age,. Two body sherds with comb decoration filled with white inlay. Fabric GAF2/LNEBA. Colour: reddish-brown throughout. Condition worn. Ashmolean Museum 1972.21–2. Unstratified.

8   **Beaker**, Late Neolithic/early Bronze Age. Body sherd (10 g) with all-over comb decoration. Fabric GA2/LNEBA. Colour: ext. reddish-brown; core black; int. yellowish-brown. Condition very worn. Context 2645.

9   **Vessel** ?early/middle Bronze Age. Four base sherds and a shoulder sherd (74 g) The shoulder sherd has two comb impressed lines. The base has multiple perforations that were made during manufacture. Fabric GF2/BA. Colour: ext. reddish-brown; core grey; int. reddish-brown. Condition average-worn. Unstratified.

LATER BRONZE AGE POTTERY
Summary of Report by Alistair Barclay

A total of 98 sherds (2.7 kg) of middle and late Bronze Age pottery in the Deverel-Rimbury and post-Deverel-Rimbury traditions was recovered, almost all of which was residual (Fig. 30). Some of the pottery could not be assigned with confidence to either one of these traditions and is classified as mid/late Bronze Age. In the Upper Thames Valley the Deverel-Rimbury style appears to go out of use by *c* 1150 cal BC, and is replaced by a range of simple ovoid and straight-sided jars and bowls. After 1000 cal BC this range of vessels is expanded to include shouldered forms such as jars, cups and bowls. By 800 cal BC there is an increase in the use of decoration which includes finger-tipping on coarseware jars and incision on fineware jars (Barclay *et al.* 2001).

A total of 20 different flint, grog, quartzite and shell tempered fabrics were identified (Table 2). In the Upper Thames Valley Deverel-Rimbury pottery was usually made from fossil shell, flint and quartzite fabrics, depending upon which was locally available. Shell temper was used less frequently over time, whilst the use of flint and quartzite increases during

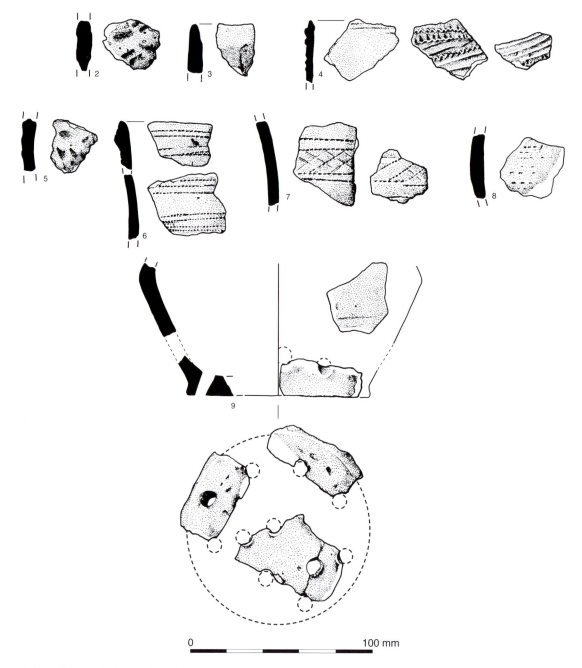

Figure 29   Other Neolithic and Beaker pottery.

the late Bronze Age. The figure of around 60% for flint/quartzite at Spring Road falls between the 49% at Eynsham (Barclay *et al.* 2001) and the arguably later site at Wallingford (Barclay 2006) where 80–90% of the pottery was flint and/or quartzite tempered.

Middle Bronze Age

Just 13 Deverel-Rimbury sherds (1264 g) were found, all in pit 1201. These sherds include a simple plain lug (Fig. 30, 5) and ten refitting sherds from a base from two Bucket Urns. The base is from a well-made, large vessel. There is a difference in the size of the flint temper used for the base and walls, that for the walls being notably much coarser (Pl. 6).

Mid/late Bronze Age

A total of 56 sherds (1121 g) can only be assigned to the mid/late Bronze Age, most of which were plain body sherds.

Late Bronze Age

A total of 29 late Bronze Age sherds (295 g), including some from ovoid or bipartite jars were found. They are mostly comparable to the early Post-Deverel-Rimbury pottery from Eynsham (Barclay *et al.* 2001) and Rams Hill (Barrett 1975, fig. 3.5), and probably date from *c* 1150–900 cal BC. There were, however, a few sherds, including one from a fine

Table 2   Later Bronze Age pottery fabrics.

Flint-tempered		
F1	hard fabric with fine angular flint	2 sherds, 6 g
F2	hard fabric with medium angular flint	6 sherds, 72 g
F3	hard fabric with coarse angular flint	18 sherds, 1520 g
FA1	hard fabric with fine angular flint and quartz sand	1 sherd, 7 g
FA2	hard fabric with medium angular flint and quartz sand	11 sherds, 113 g
FA3	hard fabric with coarse angular flint and quartz sand	1 sherd, 32 g
FG1	hard fabric with fine angular flint and rare grog	1 sherd, 14 g
Grog-tempered		
G2	soft fabric with angular grog	1 sherd, 5 g
GF1	soft fabric with fine grog and flint	1 sherd, 84 g
GQ3	soft fabric with coarse grog and quartzite	1 sherd, 27 g
GS3	soft fabric with coarse grog and coarse shell	1 sherd, 3 g
Quartzite-tempered		
Q2	hard fabric with medium angular quartzite	6 sherds, 18 g
Q3	hard fabric with coarse angular quartzite	4 sherds, 84 g
QA2	hard fabric with medium angular quartzite and quartz sand	12 sherds, 230 g
QB2	hard fabric with medium angular quartzite and black glauconitic sand	1 sherd, 2 g
Shell-tempered		
S1	Hard fabric with fine shell inclusions	1 sherd, 2 g
S2	Hard fabric with medium shell inclusions	4 sherds, 12 g
S3	Hard fabric with coarse shell inclusions	20 sherds, 399 g
SG3	Hard fabric with coarse shell inclusions and rare angular grog	1 sherd, 4 g
SQ3	Hard fabric with coarse shell inclusions and rare angular quartzite	4 sherds, 41 g

Plate 6   Wall of middle Bronze Age vessel from pit 1108, showing different tempering of base and wall.

bipartite cup or bowl and another with finger-tipped decoration from a shouldered jar, which are more comparable to the large assemblage from Wallingford (Barclay 2006), which probably dates from a later period, *c* 900–700 cal BC.

Illustrated Catalogue (Fig. 30)

1 **Plain bipartite jar**, late Bronze Age. Rim and shoulder sherd (27 g). Fabric GQ3/LBA. Colour: ext. reddish-brown; core grey; int. reddish-brown. Condition worn. Grave 3514 (7/C/17).

2 **Large bipartite jar**, late Bronze Age. Shoulder sherd (84 g). Fabric GF1/LBA. Colour: ext. reddish-brown; core black; int. reddish-brown. Condition average. Grave 3514 (7/C/17).

3 **Bipartite jar**, late Bronze Age. Finger-tip decorated shoulder sherd (5 g). Fabric Q2/LBA. Colour: ext. reddish-brown; core grey; int. brown. Condition average. Grave 3521 (10/F/4).

4 **Rim sherd** (2 g) from a **cup** or **small bowl**. Late Bronze Age. Fabric FA1/LBA. Colour: ext. brown; core black; int. brown. Condition worn. Context 1154.

5 **Simple lug** (5 g) probably from a **Bucket Urn**. Middle Bronze Age. Fabric F2/MBA. Colour: ext. brown-grey; core red; int. brown grey. Condition average to worn. Context 1180.

6 Two **refitting sherds** (48 g) from the rim of a **straight-sided** or **ovoid jar**. Late Bronze Age. Fabric/LBA. Colour: ext. buff; core black; int. grey brown. Condition average. OCMS 1994.34.

7 Two **shoulder sherds** (14 g) from a **bipartite jar** or **bowl**. Late Bronze Age. Fabric QA2/LBA. Colour: ext. brown; core & int. black. Condition worn. OCMS 1994.34.

8 **Simple rim** (14 g). Late Bronze Age. Fabric Q3/LBA. Colour: ext. black; core brown; int. grey. Condition average to worn. OCMS 1994.34.

9 **Simple rim** (6 g). Late Bronze Age. Fabric F3/LBA. Colour: ext. reddish-brown; core black; int. reddish-brown. Condition average to worn. OCMS 1994.34.

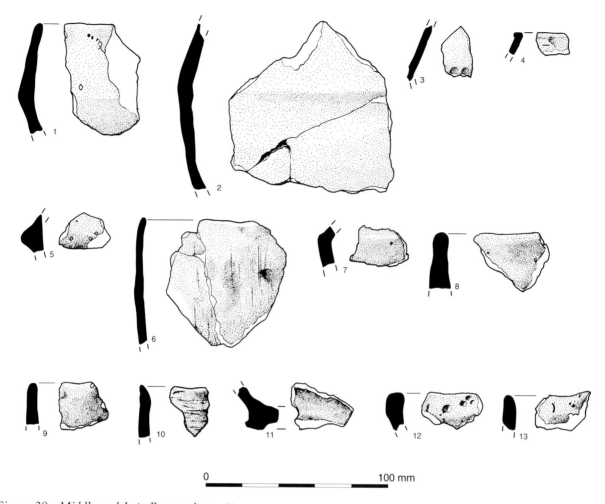

Figure 30   Middle and Late Bronze Age pottery.

10 **Simple everted rim** (3 g). Late Bronze Age. Fabric Q2/LBA. Colour: ext. brown; core & int. black. Condition average to worn. OCMS 1994.34.

11 **Three sherds** including a base (35 g). Late Bronze Age. Fabric S3/LBA. Colour: ext. pinkish red; core grey; int. grey pink. Condition worn. OCMS 1994.34 sect 11.

12 **Simple rim** (8 g). Late Bronze Age. Fabric S3/LBA. Colour: ext. orange-brown; core grey; int. brownish-grey. Condition worn. Context 704.

13 **Simple rim** (4 g). Late Bronze Age. Fabric S3/LBA. Colour: ext. mottled grey and reddish-brown; core grey; int. reddish-brown. Condition worn. Context 704.

LATER PREHISTORIC POTTERY
by Jane Timby

The later prehistoric assemblage, including material considered transitional between the later Bronze Age and early Iron Age, comprises 715 sherds weighing 6.7 kg (Fig. 31). Most sherds appear to date to the later Bronze Age-early Iron Age with a small proportion extending into the middle Iron Age period. A few sherds represent the later Iron Age. The assemblage is not well preserved and nearly half was residual.

The assemblage complements the material already published from Ashville Trading Estate (De Roche 1978) and Wyndyke Furlong (Timby 1999). Although considerably smaller, it appears to contain a distinctively earlier component. The slender ceramic evidence from Spring Road suggests that settlement in this area ceased during the earlier part of the middle Iron Age and did not recommence until the later 1st or early 2nd century AD.

Coarseware fabrics augmented by a small number of finer or decorated wares dominate the later Bronze Age/early-middle Iron Age pottery. In total some 27 fabrics were defined which fall into eight broad ware groups (Table 3). In broad terms calcareous wares dominate accounting for 52% by count, followed by sandy wares (23%), ferruginous wares (6%) and the sand and limestone group (5.5%.). Fabrics that hint at a later Bronze Age pedigree in particular, include grog and flint-tempered sherds and sandy wares. Featured sherds belonging to this phase include the biconical bowl (Fig. 31, 1), a tripartite jar (Fig. 31, 8), a shouldered jar (Fig. 31, 16) and the use of finger-pressed or slashed decoration (Fig. 31, 11, 14–5). More typical of the early Iron

Table 3. Late Bronze Age/early Iron Age and Iron Age pottery fabrics.

A	*Calcareous*	
	L1	sparse coarse fossil shell
	L2	sandy, alluvial shell
	L3	sandy, iron, alluvial shell
	L4	common fossil shell, iron
	L5	oolitic limestone
	L6	limestone some shell
	L7	sparse limestone
	L00	other limestone wares
B	*Sandy wares*	
	S1	well-sorted fine quartz
	S2	ill-sorted quartz, iron, limestone
	S3	glauconitic sand
	S4	sandy, micaceous, glauconite
	S5	ill-sorted quartz, iron, limestone
	S6	fine black sandy, iron, mica, lime
	S7	granular sandy, ill-sorted quartz
	S8	fine micaceous with iron
	S9	fine sandy, haematite imit. Slip
	S00	miscellaneous other sandy
C	*Sand and limestone*	
	SL1	sand and alluvial shell
	SL2	sand and fossil limestone
D	*Ferruginous*	
	I1	Iron rich
	I2	oolitic iron
E	*Iron- and limestone-tempered*	
	IL1	oolitic iron and limestone
	IL2	iron rich and limestone
	ISL	mixture iron, quartz and limestone
F	*Flint-tempered*	
	FI	iron rich with flint
	FIS	flint and iron in sandy matrix
G	*Grog-tempered*	
	G2	grog-tempered
H	*Grog- and limestone-tempered*	
	GL	grog and limestone-tempered
I	*Organic*	
	O2	organic with limestone
	O3	organic with quartz sand
	unclassif	
	OO	less than 10mm

Age are tripartite bowls with flaring rims and a burnished finish (Fig. 31,10 and 13), and jars with vertical walls and plain undifferentiated rims (Fig 31, 5).

Eleven decorated sherds were noted: three with finger depressions on the body (*cf.* Fig. 31.11); two with finger-tipped rims and six with incised decoration. The latter included a tripartite bowl with incised chevrons on the upper wall (Fig. 31, 4), a rim sherd with deeply incised chevrons on the rim edge (Fig. 31, 3), one bodysherd with a single curvilinear line, and one bodysherd with at least five incised

horizontal lines. Two rims had slashed diagonal lines around the rim edge (Fig. 31, 14–5). One small sandy ware sherd with a haematite slip was recovered from Iron Age grave 2126 and a sherd with an orange-red burnished finish imitating a haematite slip came from modern grave 3525.

Illustrated catalogue (Fig. 31)

1 **Biconical bowl** with a high carination, near vertical rim and a small base. Approximately 75% complete. Patchy firing. The rim is partially vitrified although it is not clear whether this is from the original firing or subsequent use. The exterior is burnished, the interior is carefully smoothed with visible tooling marks. Dark brown to reddish brown or black in colour. The underside of the base is slightly pitted and rough. Fabric FIS. Modern grave 3517.

2 **Bodysherd** with incised line decoration, probably infilled triangles. Slightly rounded profile suggesting a globular bowl. Fabric S5 but with some subangular quartz accompanying the rounded grains. Pit 1008 (secondary fill 1006).

3 **Carinated bowl** with deeply incised chevrons on the rim edge. Dark grey-brown sandy ware. Fabric S1. Redeposited in ditch 1077 (1076).

4 Two joining **bodysherds** from a **tripartite bowl** decorated with incised continuous chevrons on the upper body. Matt dark brown surfaces. Fabric S2. Pit 2299 (primary fill 2251).

5 **Rim** and joining **bodysherds**. Dark red-brown to grey in colour with an irregular external surface. Fabric L1. Pit 2299 (primary fill 2251).

6 **Sharply carinated bodysherd** from a **bowl**, dark grey in colour. Burnished on the interior and exterior surfaces, Fabric S6. Pit 2299 (2184).

7 **Rim** from a **jar** with a slightly internally beaded rim and decorated with finger depressions below the rim. Brownish- orange in colour with a hackley fracture. Fabric L1 variant with very sparse coarse shell and occasional rounded limestone. Pit 2299 (2184).

8 **Tripartite jar** or **large bowl**. A coarseware fabric, orange-brown in colour with matt surfaces. Fabric I1. Pit 2299 (2184).

9 **Flared rim fineware bowl**. Orange-red in colour with a grey core. Finely micaceous. Fabric L2. Posthole 2055 (tertiary fill 2052).

10 **Flared rim bowl**. Light brown exterior, dark grey interior. The smooth surfaces were probably originally burnished internally and externally. A finely micaceous fabric containing sparse iron, quartz sand, limestone and organic matter. Fabric FIS. Tree throw 3050 (3049).

11 **Slackly carinated sherd** with finger depressions on the carination. Fabric L1. Tree-throw hole 2113.

12 **Jar** with a finger-depressed rim broken on the lower edge at the point of a carination. Matt dark brown in colour. Fabric SL. Modern grave 3522 (11/E/14).

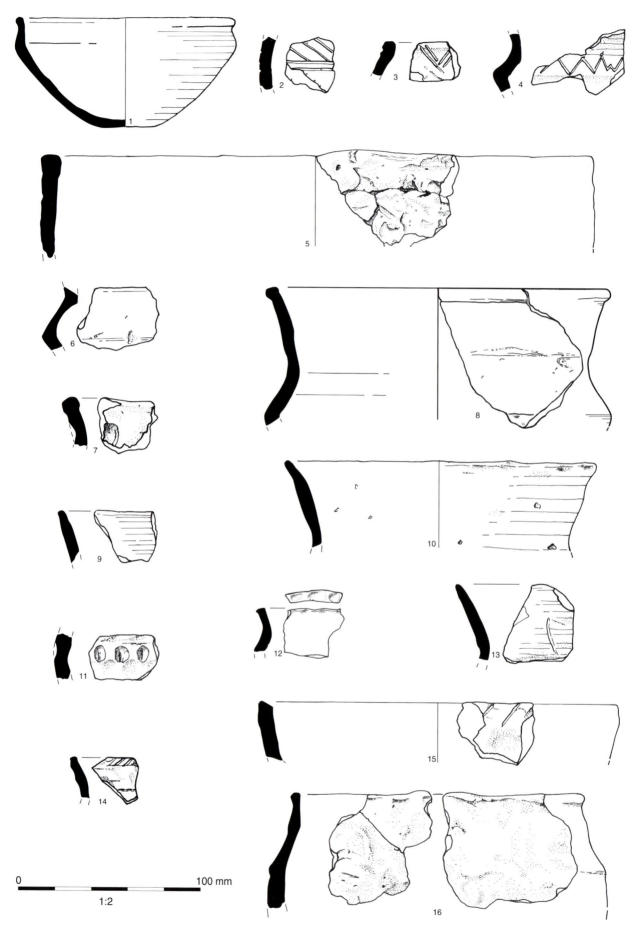

Figure 31   Late Bronze Age to Iron Age pottery.

13 **Rim** and **neck** from a **flared rim bowl**. Burnished interior and exterior surfaces. Black slightly micaceous fabric. Fabric S4. Modern grave 3522 (11/E/14).

14 **Plain, sharply everted rim** decorated with incised slashes on the outer edge. Matt dark red-brown in colour with a grey core. Fabric S7. Modern grave 3525 (10/A/9).

15 **Plain internally bevelled rim** decorated with incised slashes along the outer edge. Orange brown in colour with a grey core. Fabric L1. Modern grave 3521 (10/F/4).

16 **Crudely handmade jar** with irregular finger moulded surfaces and a slightly thickened rim. Jar with a weakly carinated shoulder, quite thin-walled. Orange-brown in colour. Fabric L1. Unstratified. Ashmolean Museum, 1972.23.

ROMAN POTTERY
by Jane Timby

The Roman assemblage comprised 647 sherds (6.17 kg) of well fragmented and generally poorly preserved pottery (Fig. 32). Most of the sherds date to the 2nd century with a sparse scatter of 3rd to 4th-century wares. The assemblage is largely composed of local products from the Oxfordshire industries (Table 4). The only imports present are two small fragments of Central Gaulish samian and two sherds of Dorset black burnished ware, suggesting a site of modest or low status. The assemblage is dominated by grey sandy wares, which account for 65.5%. Jars account for 67% by EVE followed by beakers (11.5%), bowls/dishes (10.7%), mortaria (6%) and flasks (4.8%). Jars dominate on most Roman sites, but on rural sites in particular.

Most of the Roman pottery, 466 sherds (72%), came from the two ditches crossing Area 9 (1626/ 2710 and 1627). This suggests that a focus of Roman activity is fairly close by and that these are not isolated field ditches.

Later Roman activity is sparse. Only five sherds of Oxford colour-coated ware, which generally signal occupation from the second half of the 3rd century through to the later 4th century, came from the site and of these only two were stratified. The Saxon and later features on the site produced 38 sherds of redeposited Roman pottery and 58 sherds of later prehistoric date.

The shorter duration of occupation at Spring Road contrasts with the development at Ashville/Wyndyke Furlong where occupation seems to have continued from the Iron Age into the late Roman period.

Illustrated catalogue (Fig. 32)

1 **White globular beaker** with sharply out-turned rim similar to Young (1977) form W37. Decorated with orange slip. Fabric OXF WHF. Ditch 1077 (1076).

2 **Cordoned bowl** decorated with a zone of burnished line decoration. Fabric OXF RE. Ditch 1077 (1076).

3 **Whiteware mortaria**, Young (1977) type M1. Stamped either side of the spout with a double-line illiterate stamp. Ditch 1077 (1076).

4 **Handmade fossil shell-tempered jar**. Fabric: C10. Ditch 1077 (1076).

Table 4   Roman pottery fabrics.

National Fabric code	OA code		
Import			
CGSAM	S30	Central Gaulish samian	2 sherds, 5 g
Regional			
DORBB1	B11	Dorset black burnished ware	2 sherds, 24 g
Local			
OXF FR	R10/11	Oxfordshire reduced ware (fine)	281 sherds, 1891 g
OXF RE	R21	Oxfordshire reduced ware (medium-coarse)	158 sherds, 1484 g
OXF FO	O11	Oxfordshire oxidised ware (fine)	18 sherds, 83 g
OXF OX	O21	Oxfordshire oxidised ware (medium-coarse)	6 sherds, 51 g
OXF RS	F51	Oxfordshire colour-coated ware	4 sherds, 73 g
OXF RSM	M41	Oxfordshire colour-coated mortaria	1 sherds, 10 g
OXF WHF	W12	Oxfordshire whiteware (fine)	30 sherds, 210 g
OXF WH	W22	Oxfordshire white ware (medium-coarse)	51 sherds, 562 g
OXF WHM	M22	Oxfordshire whiteware mortaria	5 sherds, 707 g
OXF WS	Q21	Oxfordshire white-slipped ware	36 sherds, 110 g
OXF BWH	W23	Oxfordshire burnt whiteware	18 sherds, 569 g
SHELL	C10	shelly ware	4 sherds, 50 g
OXF GR		Oxfordshire grog-tempered storage jar	13 sherds, 219 g
GROG	E80	miscellaneous grog-tempered	9 sherds, 52 g
GROG1		wheelmade grog-tempered	2 sherds, 6 g
GREY00		miscellaneous Roman	7 sherds, 66 g
			647 sherds, 6172 g

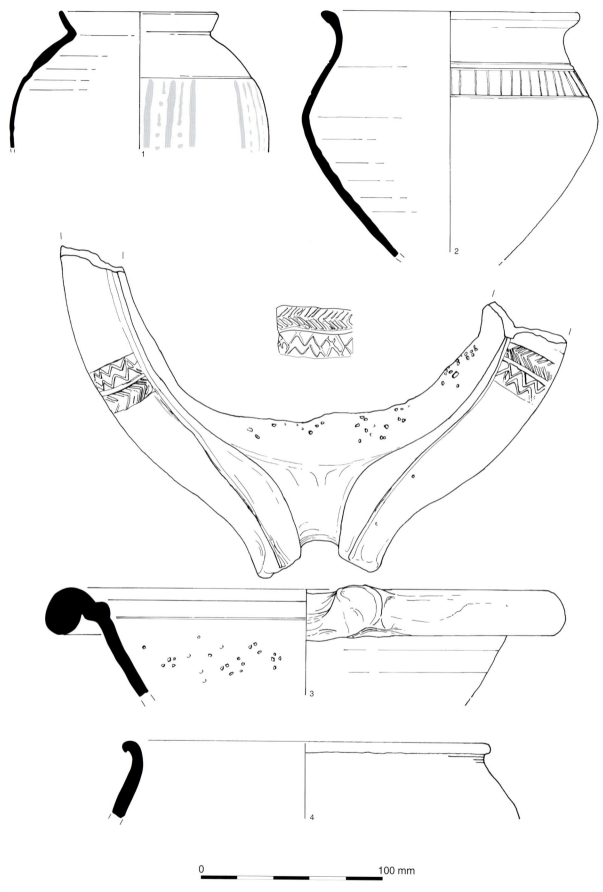

Figure 32   Roman pottery.

POST-ROMAN POTTERY
by Paul Blinkhorn

The early to middle Anglo-Saxon assemblage (Figs 35–8) consists of 680 sherds (10,431 g, EVE = 4.36), and the medieval and early post-medieval assemblage of 111 sherds (902 g, EVE = 0.05). The rest of the post-Roman pottery dates from the late 19th-century (183 sherds, 9087 g).

The range of early to middle Anglo-Saxon pottery fabrics is typical of the region and are described in Table 5. The calcareous gravels of the second terrace and the Lower Greensand deposits at Bagley Wood seem the most likely sources for the bulk of the

potting clays (Blinkhorn forthcoming), although an alternative source of greensand outcrops on Culham Heights just south of Abingdon.

The range of Anglo-Saxon vessel forms was extremely basic. Only simple bowl and jar forms were noted, with chaff-tempered fabrics less commonly used for bowls than for jars. The chaff-tempered jars had a larger mean rim diameter than the sand-tempered vessels, suggesting that the former were larger, and had a different function, perhaps as water jars (Figs 33–4).

The decorated pottery comprised stamped wares, showing that there was domestic occupation at the site during the 6th century. Fifth-century types were

Table 5   Anglo-Saxon pottery fabrics.

F1	*Fine quartz*	Moderate to dense sub-angular quartz up to 0.5 mm. Rare calcareous material of the same size and shape	236 sherds, 2760 g, EVE = 1.52
F2	*Quartz and chaff*	Sparse to moderate subrounded quartz up to 2 mm, sparse to moderate chaff voids	168 sherds, 3170 g, EVE = 1.38
F3	*Coarse quartz*	Moderate to dense subrounded quartz up to 3 mm. Rare calcareous material of the same size	20 sherds, 289 g, EVE = 0
F4	*Calcareous quartz*	Sparse to moderate sub-rounded calcareous material up to 1 mm. Sparse subrounded quartz up to 0.5 mm. Sparse chaff voids and fine silver mica	5 sherds, 40 g, EVE = 0.03
F5	*Ironstone*	Sparse to moderate rounded red ironstone up to 3 mm. Sparse quartz up to 0.5 mm, rare flint up to 5 mm	1 sherd, 6 g, EVE = 0
F6	*Chaff*	no other visible inclusions	250 sherds, 4166 g, EVE = 1.43

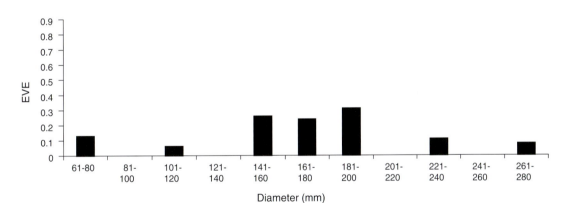

Figure 33   Saxon pottery: Jar rim diameter occurrence, for sand-tempered fabric, by EVE per diameter category.

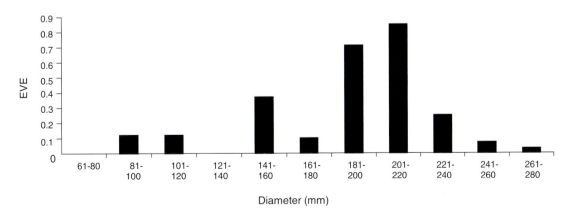

Figure 34   Saxon pottery: Jar rim diameter occurrence, for chaff-tempered fabrics, by EVE per diameter category.

entirely absent. Similarly, there is no diagnostic ceramic evidence for occupation during the middle or late Saxon periods. The medieval pottery shows that occupation in the vicinity of the site began again around the time of the Norman conquest, and continued almost until the present day.

Over half of the Anglo-Saxon pottery assemblage (by weight) derived from the two sunken-floored buildings (SFBs) excavated in 2000. SFB 2687 produced an assemblage of 293 sherds (4727 g, EVE = 2.27; Figs 35–7). The sherds were largely plain. The decorated pottery comprised a group of stamped and incised sherds, seven small incised sherds, and two rusticated sherds. This whole group suggests a date no earlier than the 6th century for the back-filling of the feature. SFB 2008 produced considerably less pottery (55 sherds, 1025 g), and none of it was decorated (Fig. 37). This could mean that the feature dates to the 7th century, but the assemblage is too small to be certain. Further significant groups were found in modern graves (Fig. 38). A group of vitrified sherds from grave 6/C/16 is worthy of note. Although their condition might be the result of other factors, this could be evidence of domestic pottery production.

Most of the excavated Anglo-Saxon sites in and around Abingdon have produced 5th-century pottery, although generally in small quantities. Such pottery was noted at Barrow Hills, Radley (Blinkhorn 2007), Barton Court Farm (Miles 1986, fiche 7), Audlett Drive (Underwood-Keevill 1992), The Vineyard (Allen 1990), and the Saxton Road cemetery (Leeds and Harden, 1936). It would seem therefore that the Spring Road cemetery area was, during the Anglo-Saxon period, largely peripheral until the 6th century.

Illustrated catalogue (Figs 35–8)

SFB 2687 (Figs 35–7)

1 **Stamped and incised sherds**. F1. Dark grey fabric with variegated grey and brown surfaces. Context 2672 and 2673 (SFB).

2 **Stamped and incised sherds**. F1. Uniform black fabric with lightly burnished outer surface. Contexts 2672, 2673 and 2703.

3 **Rusticated sherds**. F6. Dark grey fabric with light reddish-brown outer surface. Contexts 2672, 3511 (4/M/7) and 'from the OXCHS'.

4 **Rusticated sherd**. F6. Uniform dark grey fabric with lighter outer surface. Context 2703.

5 **Jar with fragment of upright, rim-mounted lug**. F1. Dark grey fabric with variegated reddish-brown and grey surfaces. Outer surface evenly burnished. Context 2672.

6 **Rim sherd from small jar**. F1. Uniform black fabric, lightly burnished outer surface. Context 2672.

7 **Rim sherd from vessel with pierced longitudinal lug on the shoulder**. F2. Dark grey fabric with slightly browner, smoothed outer surface. Context 2673.

8 **Rim sherd from jar**. F6. Dark grey fabric with unfinished surfaces. Context 2673.

9 **Rim sherd from jar**. F6. Uniform black fabric, browner on rim, smoothed surfaces. Context 2673.

10 **Shouldered jar**, shoulder and neck. F1. Black fabric with browner, lightly-burnished outer surfaces. Context 2673.

11 **Rim sherd from a jar**. F6. Uniform dark grey fabric with a smoothed outer surface. Context 2703.

12 **Base sherd**. F6. Uniform black fabric with light brown, unfinished outer surface. Patches of burnt black residue on the inner surface. Context 2703.

SFB 2008 (Fig. 37)

13 **Large bowl**, large sherd from. F2. Uniform black fabric, patches of sooting on the burnished outer surface. Context 2010.

14 **Rim sherd from jar**. F2. Uniform black fabric with browner outer surfaces. Context 2479.

Other Groups (Fig. 38)

1 **Globular jar**, upper portion of. F6. Uniform black fabric, brown patch on the smoothed, evenly burnished outer surface. Modern grave 3512 (4/M/8)

2 **Stamped and incised vessel**. F1. Uniform black fabric, burnished surfaces. 'From the OCMS'

3 **Stamped and incised vessel**. F6. Uniform greyish-brown fabric, burnished outer surface. 'From the OXCMS'

4 **Rim sherd from jar**. F1. Slightly warped, with extensive vitrification and some cracking on the outer surface. Modern Grave 3513 (6/C/16).

5 **Rim sherd from a jar**. F6. Uniform black fabric with lightly burnished surfaces. Modern Grave 3501 (3/E/32).

6 **Bowl rim sherd**. F2. Uniform dark grey fabric, smoothed outer surface. Modern grave 3501 (3/E/32).

7 **Stamped and incised vessel**. F2. Uniform dark grey fabric, smoothed outer surface. Modern grave 3530 (3/O/6).

STAMPED SAXON SHERDS
by Diane Briscoe

The Archive of Anglo-Saxon Pottery Stamps covers the period from *c* AD 325 to *c* AD 725, and maintains a database, comprising over 23,000 examples, of stamped designs on Anglo-Saxon pottery both as casts and on index cards. The database was used to compare the stamps from Spring Road with those from other sites. There are five stamp-producing sites within modern Abingdon: Saxton Road (28 stamps), Radley Road (6), Barton Court Farm (11), Barrow Hills, Radley (90), and Spring Road. The Spring Road site has produced four groups of stamped sherds, displaying eight different motifs (Figs 35 and 38). Within an approximately 15-mile

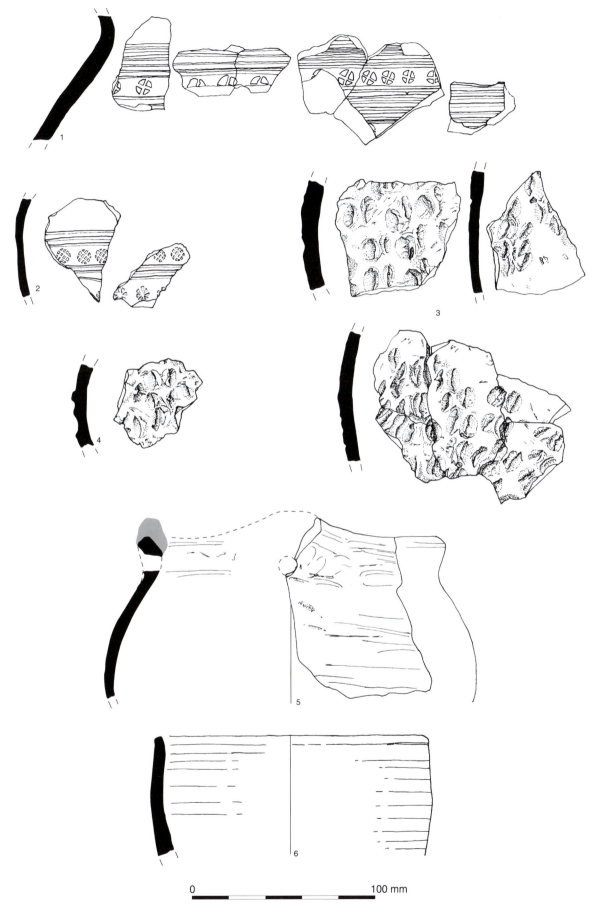

Figure 35   Saxon pottery from SFB 2687: Nos 1–6.

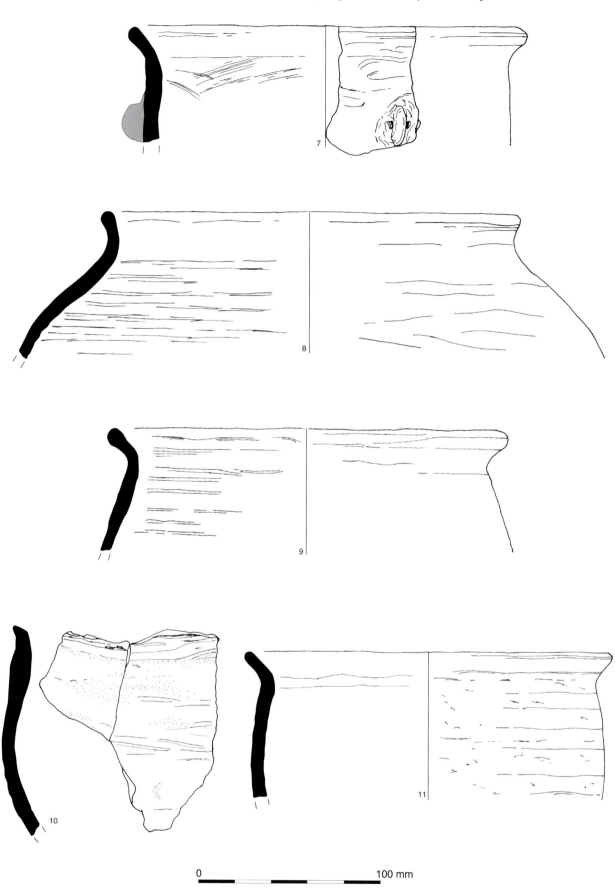

0   100 mm

Figure 36   Saxon pottery from SFB 2687: Nos 7–11.

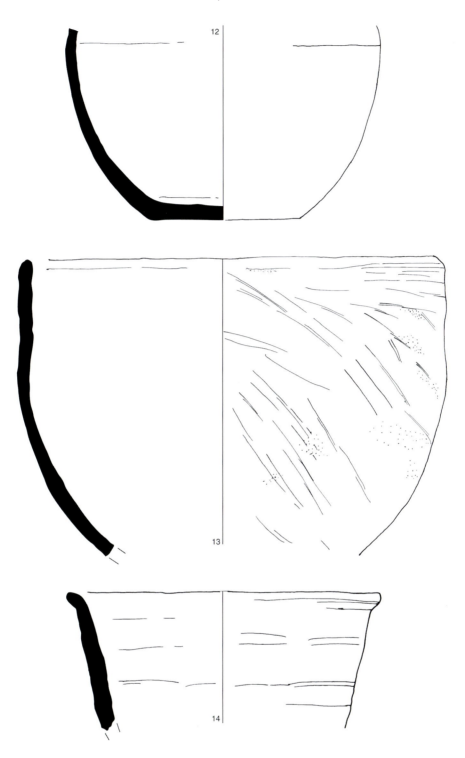

Figure 37   Saxon pottery from SFB 2687: No. 12; from SFB 2008: Nos 13–14.

radius of the site, there are another 15 sites which have produced stamps, yielding a total of 292 stamps for comparison.

Category A includes all circular stamps. *A 2ai* describes two negative rings of equal proportions. This motif is extremely common and widely distributed. Comparable local examples come from Frilford, Sutton Courtenay and Wallingford. The Frilford example, on a globular bowl, is associated with *C 3ai* and *G 2bi* stamps.

The *A 3a* group includes all circular grid stamps. *A 3aii* and *A 3aiii* describe negative grids of 3 × 3 squares and 3 × 4 squares respectively. The *A 3aii* group is reasonably common, and widely distributed. Locally, there is one much larger parallel from Cassington.

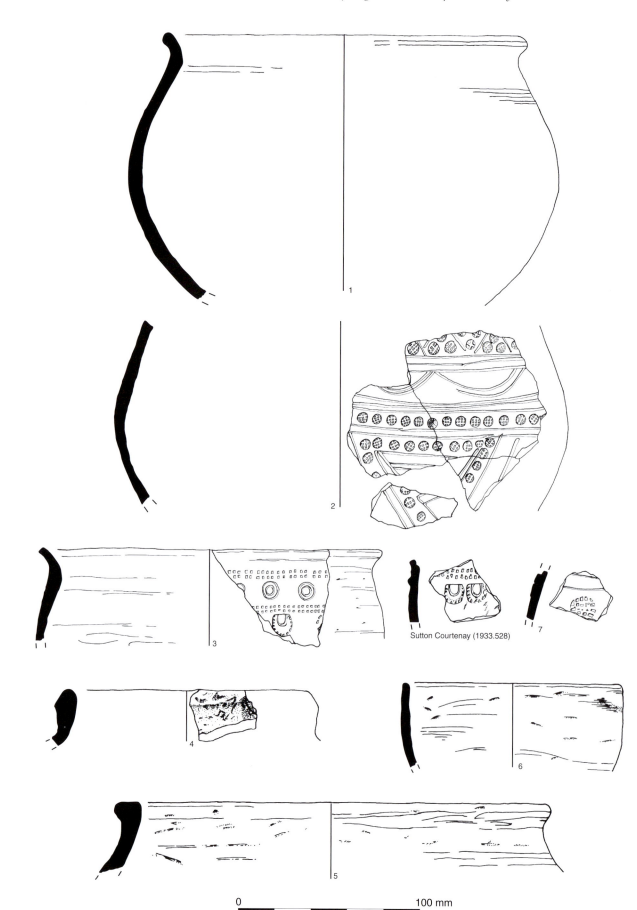

Sutton Courtenay (1933.528)

0   100 mm

Figure 38   Other Saxon pottery: Nos 1–7, plus stamped sherd from Sutton Courtenay.

Table 6 Saxon pottery: Stamped designs by type.

Briscoe Type	Size (mm)	Ref. No.	Figure
A 2ai	10 × 10	1994.29	Fig. 38, 3
A 3aii	6 × 6	1994.29	Fig. 38, 2
A 3aiii	7 × 6.5	89.121/2703	Fig. 35, 2
A 3aiii	14 × 13?	U/S	Fig. 38, 7
A 4ai	8 × 8	89.121/2672	Fig. 35, 1
A 4ai	4 × 4.5	1994.29	Fig. 38, 2
A 4aiv	13 × 12?	89.121/2672	Fig. 35, 1
A 5aviii	8 × 8.5	89.121/2703	Fig. 35, 2
C 3ai	4.5 × 4	1994.29	Fig. 38, 3
G 2bi	11 × 11	1994.29	Fig. 38, 3

The *A 3aiii* motif is also reasonably common, and widely distributed. Locally, the smaller stamp has a parallel from Sutton Courtenay, and larger examples from Radley Road, Cassington, Long Wittenham and Sutton Courtenay. The second *A 3aiii* is comparable to the Cassington stamp, but is not from the same die. Its two closest local parallels are from Eynsham Abbey.

The *A 4ai* motif – the 'hot-cross-bun' – is extremely common and very widely distributed. The smaller stamp has parallels from Eynsham Abbey and Radley Road. The second is a very common size. Locally, there are eight parallels from Barrow Hills (3), Eynsham Abbey (1), Kingsey (2) and Sutton Courtenay (3).

The *A 4aiv* motif is a 'hot-cross-bun' stamp with a small circle where the positive arms of the cross meet. This is an uncommon motif, and all parallels are from East Anglia, the Midlands or Yorkshire. It is the largest recorded; the next largest comes from West Keal, Lincolnshire.

Motif *A 5aviii* is a circular negative rosette with eight petals – a very common motif with a wide distribution. Locally, there are two parallels from Sutton Courtenay, with different sized examples from Eynsham Abbey (2), and Barrow Hills (2).

Category C includes all square and rectangular stamps. Motif *C 3ai* describes an open-ended positive upright cross on a negative rectangle. There are five much larger local examples from Eynsham Abbey.

Category G includes half-circle, crescent and horse-shoe stamps. *G 2bi* describes a segmented negative horseshoe with negative inner horseshoe. This is an uncommon motif with a wide distribution. A sherd from Sutton Courtenay in the Ashmolean Museum (published in Leeds 1947, Plate XXII b) has a 'like' stamp, that is it was made by the same die (see Fig. 38, Sutton Courtenay, 1933.528). This is a very rare occurrence. Other parallels come from Spong Hill, Norfolk; Staines, Surrey; and Mucking, Essex, but were made by different dies.

Most of the stamps are common motifs from which little can be deduced. The motifs from Spring Road overlap with only 11 of the 19 local sites, although some sites have produced fairly rare stamps. It seems fairly definite that Spring Road's closest links are with Sutton Courtenay, lying downstream, not with any of the other Abingdon sites. It should

be noted that there are also parallels, although less close, between Spring Road and Eynsham Abbey.

The identification of a 'like' stamp is very exciting. The Archive holds only 10 or 12 examples of 'like' stamps from different sites, and they are fairly rare even within a site. The very small number of 'like' stamps would appear to indicate that pottery was generally produced locally using dies manufactured by individuals in each settlement. I am also quite certain that individual potters had a number of dies of the same stamp type, varying in size. However, a couple of the 'like' stamps have been found on sites many miles apart, which would indicate trade or travel between them. The presence of a 'like' stamp on pots from these two sites certainly indicates a link between them.

FIRED CLAY
Summaries of reports by Jane Timby and Alistair Barclay

Neolithic fired clay

In total 15 fragments (203 g) of fired clay came from Grooved Ware pit 2622 (fills 2619–20). The fired clay was made generally from a coarse sandy clay, and included a number of small slab-like pieces with either rough or smooth surfaces. One piece had two finger-tip impressions on its oxidised outer surface (Pl. 7). These fragments are too well fired to be daub. They could derive from an oven or hearth structure or have been used as props for the firing of pottery. Similar fragments were recovered from a Grooved Ware pit at Barrow Hills, Radley (Barclay and Halpin 1999, 82).

Iron Age fired clay

The fired clay from Iron Age contexts comprised nine fragments of poorly-fired, orange, sandy textured possible pit or hearth lining from a deposit (2309) which lay next to posthole 2307 (and seemed to have formed when it still contained a post), and half a spherical spindlewhorl with a central perforation (Fig. 13) that had been burnt, from the upper fill (2200) of Grave 2197. It has a diameter of 44 mm, and is 34 mm high. The object is made from poorly-wedged, slightly sandy clay containing sparse fossil shell and iron inclusions.

Roman fired clay

Roman contexts produced 48 fragments of fired clay mainly in a dark red fabric with sparse limestone and organic matter. None of the fragments was featured.

Saxon fired clay

The 23 pieces of fired clay from Saxon contexts showed no indication of form or function, apart from one wattle impression. The fired clay had a fine, powdery texture, buff in colour, with no visible inclusions. Most came from sunken-featured buildings,

Plate 7   Fired clay with finger-nail impressions from Grooved Ware pit 2619.

suggesting a structural function. A possible fragment of Roman tile was found in sunken-featured building 2008.

ANALYSIS OF A COPPER AWL
Summary of report by Peter Northover

A copper awl (Fig. 7) was found alongside the upper legs of the burial in the Beaker grave (3037) which was radiocarbon dated to 2460–2200 cal BC (see Chap. 5). The awl has an asymmetrical lozenge profile and is rectangular in cross-section. It is 63.5 mm long and 4.0 mm wide at its widest point. Both ends are blunt points. The shorter end may have been reworked.

Lozenge-shaped awls are generally found in Beaker contexts, usually with burials. Similar awls have recently been found with Step 6 Beakers in south Wales (Ehrenberg 1982; Brassil unpublished data) where they have been radiocarbon dated to c 2200–1900 cal BC. They have also been found with burial A, Amesbury 51 and at Radley (Needham in Barclay and Halpin 1999, 188–92 and table 7.8), both of which have been dated to c 2330–1950 cal BC.

Electron probe microanalysis has shown that the Spring Road awl is made of slightly impure copper, with 0.46% total impurities. The principal impurities are silver (0.13%), nickel (0.15%) and antimony (0.08%). Few other awls have been analysed, but comparisons are possible with two analysed copper examples, both from burials in Hampshire (see 'Detailed report').

In general the impurity patterns of early copper objects in Britain fall into two groups (Northover 1999). The first group is characterised by a very consistent pattern containing arsenic, antimony and silver. This group has an Irish origin and is typical of copper axes. The second group, to which the Spring Road awl belongs, is more heterogeneous, and often contains nickel as an impurity. Much of the metal in the second group probably derives from the continent. Objects in this group include two rings from Barrow Hills which have a radiocarbon date of 2700–2100 cal BC, and probably belong to the same early horizon as the Spring Road awl. Because copper is so easily reworked it need not be the case that the metal was imported in its finished form, and it is likely that the earliest metal-working in southern England consisted of the reprocessing of small items of imported copper.

ROMAN COINS
by Paul Booth

Three Roman coins were recovered. All are typical issues of the second half of the 4th century AD but none can be precisely dated.

1   **AE4. Imitation FEL TEMP REP falling horseman type.** *c* AD 353–360. Ditch 1627, context 1098.
2   **AE3. Valens. SECURITAS REIPUBLICAE with victory advancing left.** Probably Trier but mint mark illegible in detail. AD 364–378. Ditch 1626, context 1154.
3   **AE3. Gratian. Probably GLORIA NOVI SAECULI with standing figure of emperor holding labarum.** Arles, but mint mark not clear. AD 367–375. The coin has been pierced, presumably for

reuse in the Anglo-Saxon period, as it was found in a pit containing only Saxon pottery. Unstratified find from grave digging.

OTHER METAL OBJECTS
Summary of report by Leigh Allen and Martin Henig

A small assemblage of 10 copper alloy objects, 52 iron objects and 1 lead object have been recovered from the excavation and recent grave digging. Most of these consistent of unidentifiable fragments or undiagnostic items such as nails, many of which were found in contexts such as the Victorian quarry, tree-throw holes and the topsoil.

The more interesting objects include a Roman copper alloy disc brooch, found in Saxon pit 245. The centre of the brooch rises to a cupped stub and two incised grooves run around the inside of the raised rim. There are also six plain lugs on the outside of the disc. The hinge and catch plate survive. The brooch had been perforated and may have been suspended. A perforated Roman coin was found in the same pit. Close parallels have been found at Wakerley, Northamptonshire (Butcher 1978, 218–220, fig. 57, no. 6) and at Kidlington (Hunter and Kirk 1952/3, 57, fig. 25, no. 2) where a 2nd–3rd century date was suggested.

The remaining finds include the circular spatulate end of an unstratified copper alloy Roman unguent spoon or ear scoop, and a large copper alloy pin with a spherical wire-wound head which was found during grave digging next to the shoulder of an extended burial. Such pins were used from the 13th century onwards but were most common in the 16th and 17th centuries.

WORKED BONE OBJECTS (Fig. 39)
Summary of report by Leigh Allen and Tim Allen, with bone identifications by Emma Jayne Evans

A total of six worked or utilised bone objects have been have been found as a result of excavation and recent grave digging. The most striking of these was a gouge or hide scraper made from part of the mid shaft of a pig tibia found in posthole 2373 in the timber circle (Pl. 8). This bone has been radiocarbon dated to 1520–1310 cal BC. The ends of the bone are missing and it has been gnawed but several areas of polish are still evident. The production of such an artefact from pig bone is rare, probably because pig bone is more porous and liable to split than the bone of other species (Seager Smith in Lawson 2000, 222–40). Pig bone is, however, frequently associated with late Neolithic monuments and pits, and its use here might have been related to the timber circle.

A plain, highly polished bone finger ring (Fig. 10) made from a large mammal long bone was found in front of the head of the middle Iron Age burial of a 4–5 year old child (2125). The ring has a circular cross section and measures 24 mm in diameter (16 mm internal diameter). No exact parallels for this ring have been found, although rings of copper alloy, iron and shale have been found associated with Iron Age burials in Yorkshire (Stead 1991, 208–10 and 218–20), and a bone toggle was found behind the head of a male burial at Gravelly Guy, Stanton Harcourt, Oxfordshire (Lambrick and Allen 2004, Fig. 6.1).

The remaining objects include an unstratified fragment from the central tooth segment of a double sided comb (Fig. 39, 1), probably of antler, two highly polished bone points made from splinters of mammal longbones (Fig. 39, 2), one unstratified,

0   50 mm

Figure 39   Worked bone objects.

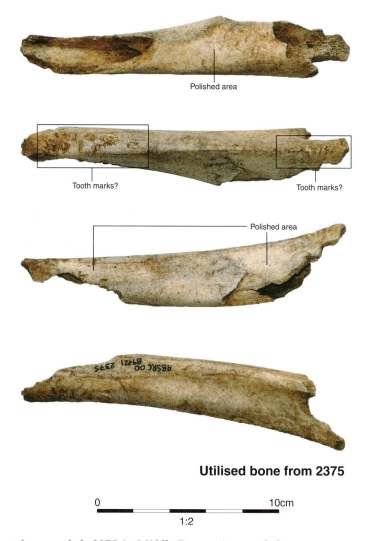

Polished area

Tooth marks?

Tooth marks?

Polished area

Utilised bone from 2375

0   10cm

1:2

Plate 8   Bone implement from posthole 2375 in Middle Bronze Age posthole arc.

the other from a tree-throw hole (2347), and an unstratified antler point (Fig. 39, 3).

GLASS
Summary of report by Rachel Tyson

Two globular glass beads, one blue and one turquoise, were found as a result of recent grave digging. Their original context is unknown. Globular monochrome cobalt blue beads were common from the Roman through to the early Medieval period and also occur in the Iron Age. Turquoise beads are less common, and are more likely to date from the Saxon period, making it likely that this example dates from the 5th–7th centuries.

Chapter 4: The Environmental Evidence

HUMAN SKELETAL ASSEMBLAGE
Summary by Ceridwen Boston of report by Peter Hacking and Angela Boyle

The human bone assemblage comprised a young female skeleton (3036) dating to the Beaker period, and four middle Iron Age skeletons (2125a, 2125b, 2199 and 2243) interred within three purpose-cut graves. Bone preservation was good to very good and all, bar infant skeleton 2125b, were nearly complete.

Beaker burial

A shallow subrectangular grave in Area 5 contained the intact remains of a young adult female, aged 20–24 years. A radiocarbon date of 2460–2200 BC (95% confidence) was obtained from the skeleton. She was crouched on her right side on a south-east – north-west orientation. A copper awl – the only artefact in the grave – was positioned alongside her upper legs. She was 1.52 m (4′ 9″) tall, and, during childhood, had suffered from iron deficiency anaemia – manifested as mild cribra orbitalia in the right eye orbit. This condition was relatively common in the Neolithic and Bronze Age, affecting approximately 13.8% and 10% of the population respectively (Roberts and Cox 2003, 67 and 85). Of the 32 Neolithic and Bronze Age inhumations from nearby Barrow Hills, Radley, three (9%) displayed this deficiency (Boyle in Barclay and Halpin 1999, 172–3). The most common probable causes were an inadequate dietary intake of iron and chronic blood loss through intestinal parasitism (Stuart-Macadam 1991, 102–3). Dental enamel hypoplasia (a thinning of the dental enamel), an indicator of episodes of poor nutrition (possibly seasonal food shortages) and/or disease in early childhood, was present on a number of tooth crowns.

Middle Iron Age burials

A cluster of three purpose-cut graves was found in Area 8 within the confines of, but probably post-dating, a roundhouse. These contained the articulated skeletons of two young adult males (2199 and 2243), aged 19–21 years and 20–24 years respectively, and a 4–5 year old child (2125a). All were radiocarbon dated to the 3–4th centuries cal BC. Some bones of a three month old infant (2125b) were discovered in the backfill of the child's grave.

Child 2125a was orientated south-east – north-west, and was crouched on its right side with the legs tightly flexed. A bone ring was found near the skull. Skeleton 2199 was positioned in a half-sitting position, lying supine with the back raised against

the northern edge of the grave. A fragmentary spindle whorl was retrieved from the backfill but this may not have been directly associated with the burial. Skeleton 2243 had been laid out crouched and prone, on a north-south alignment. A later circular feature (2454) may have removed most of the skull and upper vertebrae (or, alternatively, have been cut to accommodate the head which was removed in some other way). Both adults were of average height for the period (1.70 m and 1.68 m). Skeleton 2199 showed evidence of trauma: a united fracture of the left fifth metacarpal, and a possible puncture wound to the left distal femur with secondary periostitis. He also displayed marked dental disease: three caries and two abscesses. Skeleton 2243 had osteochondritis dissecans of the left femoral condyle – an indicator of strenuous physical activity in adolescence or youth (Aufderheide and Rodríguez-Martin 1998).

Two other crouched inhumations were exhumed by modern grave diggers in the vicinity, and although undated, they may well have formed part of this burial group. Burial groups within purpose-cut graves are rare in the Iron Age, although a group of 35 unaccompanied inhumations at Yarnton, Oxfordshire, have also been radiocarbon dated to the 3–4th centuries cal BC (Hey *et al.* 1999).

ANIMAL BONES
Summary of report by Bethan Charles

A total of 2123 hand-collected fragments of animal bone and 1745 fragments from sieving was recovered. The majority of the bones were in good condition. Many, particularly those from Anglo-Saxon contexts, had butchery marks, and a small number had been burnt. The only concentration of burnt bone, however, was in late Neolithic pit 2622. Many bone fragments had canine tooth marks (Plate 8).

Most of the bone from Neolithic pit 2622 was pig, with a small amount from sheep and cattle (the latter consisting mostly of teeth and rib fragments). Two of the pig mandibles indicate an age at death of between 7 and 14 months. The scapula of a very young pig was also identified. The predominance of pig bone in this pit fits the pattern from other Grooved Ware pits in the Upper Thames and beyond (Grigson 1982). Whether this reflects the importance of pig in the economy or their particular ceremonial significance is uncertain (*cf.* Levitan and Serjeantson in Barclay and Halpin 1999, 239).

Sheep and cattle bones, although in very small numbers, were the main species from late Bronze Age, Iron Age and Roman features. Pig bones were present only in the Roman deposits and from sieved Iron Age deposits. Horse bones were recovered from both the Iron Age and Roman deposits including a metatarsal from a Roman pit (2299) with knife marks around the proximal articulation. Of the dog bones identified in the Roman deposits two were skull fragments (found within pit 2650 and ditch 1627). No butchery marks were identified on the dog bones.

The small number of bones identified from the late Bronze Age, Iron Age and Roman features do not provide much information regarding the site's economy. Sheep and cattle appear to have provided the majority of the meat, as they seem to have done at Ashville Trading Estate just across the Larkhill Stream (Wilson 1978).

The majority of the animal bone from the site came from Saxon deposits, mostly from sunken-featured buildings 2008 and 2687. The deposits consisted largely of butchery refuse (skull, foot bones, vertebrae and ribs) from cattle, sheep and pigs. Most Anglo-Saxon assemblages show cattle and sheep to be the dominant species (Bourdillon and Coy 1980; Crabtree 1994), although it has been suggested by Clutton-Brock (1979) that pigs were more common on small-holdings. Tooth wear indicates that most of the cattle were killed as young animals, suggesting that only a small number were kept until adulthood, with the majority raised for meat and killed whilst young. Some of the sheep were also killed at an early age, perhaps as part of a cull to reduce the size of the flock over the winter. However, some animals were kept until much older, as breeding stock and for their milk, wool and dung. All of the pig bones came from young animals, usually less than one year old.

Four fragments of Red deer antler were found in Saxon deposits, all of which had knife marks, and were probably waste from working. A comb (Fig. 39, 1) and a pin-beater (Fig. 39, 3) made from antler were found. A single fragment of dog bone was also found.

SMALL ANIMAL REMAINS
by Mark Nokkert

During the excavations 114 small animal remains were collected, consisting of bones of pine marten, house mouse, water vole, domestic fowl, domestic goose, blackbird, frog, toad and eel. Remains of domestic fowl and goose dominate the assemblage. The two pine marten bones came from the fill of a late Neolithic pit. Except for a single domestic fowl bone from a 13th-century context, all the other remains belonged to the early to middle Saxon period. The majority of these came from the fill of two sunken-featured buildings dated to the 6th century AD. On a few of the domestic geese remains butchery marks were noticed. With the exception of the remains of domestic fowl, domestic geese, the single eel bone and possibly also the blackbird bone, the remains of all other species can be considered as accidental

intrusions and were probably not deposited as a result of human consumption. Despite an extensive sieving program carried out on site, the near-complete lack of fish and other wild animals in the assemblage suggests that wild animal remains played an insignificant role in the diet of the Saxon inhabitants of this site. This is in agreement with the results of the analysis of the larger animal remains from this site.

CHARRED PLANT REMAINS
by Mark Robinson

Extensive sampling was undertaken for charred plant remains during the excavation. The concentrations of remains were mostly low but the charred plant remains from six samples, and the charcoal from 17 samples were analysed in full. Small quantities of *Corylus avellana* (hazel) nut shell fragments, a couple of cereal grasses and mixed charcoal of *Quercus* sp. (oak), hazel and Pomoideae (hawthorn, apple etc) were found in two samples from a Grooved Ware pit (2622). A mixed range of charcoal including *Fagus sylvatica* (beech) was found in the Roman samples. The concentration of charred remains in samples from the two sunken-featured buildings was, at around one item per litre, relatively high for early Saxon contexts. The majority were cereal grains, with two crops identified with certainty: a short-grained free-threshing variety of *Triticum* sp. (rivet or bread wheat) and hulled *Hordeum vulgare* (six-row hulled barley). A few grains of *Avena* sp. were also present but it is uncertain whether they were from wild or cultivated oats. Chaff was absent apart from a rachis of *Hordeum* sp. Other food plants were represented by nut shell fragments of *Corylus avellana* and seeds of a large legume, probably either *Vicia faba* (bean) or *Pisum sativum* (pea). Weed seeds were abundant in the samples from the Saxon sunken-featured buildings. They were mostly from species which readily occur as arable weeds including *Brassica rapa* ssp. *campestris* (wild turnip), *Vicia* or *Lathyrus* sp. (vetch or tare) and *Rumex* sp. (dock) but some seeds of wet-ground plants including *Eleocharis* sp. (spike rush) were also present. The samples from the Saxon building were very rich in charcoal, mostly Pomoideae sp. but *Quercus* was also well represented.

Discussion

The predominance of hazel nut shell fragments amongst the food plant remains in the late Neolithic pit falls into the usual pattern for Grooved Ware pits although there is much debate about the importance of nuts in the diet (Robinson 2000). The crop species identified from the Saxon sunken-featured buildings were all important in the Upper Thames Valley during the early Saxon period (Robinson and Wilson 1987, 75). Hulled wheat was absent from the Saxon deposits at Spring Road even though spelt wheat was noted in a Roman ditch. There is no evidence as

Plate 9   Layer of soil with distinctive pinkish hue at the north baulk of Area 9; note also the infill of Evaluation Trench D.

yet for the continuation of *Triticum spelta* (spelt wheat) in the region beyond the end of the Roman period. Indeed, the transition from hulled to free-threshing wheat seems to have been very abrupt. However, recent discoveries point to a Saxon revival in the cultivation of *Triticum dicoccum* (emmer wheat) in the Thames Valley (Pelling and Robinson 2000). The charcoal suggests the availability of both wood-land and scrub sources of fuel from the late Neolithic to Saxon periods. The Roman record of beech is interesting because although the discovery of beech charcoal at the Abingdon Causewayed Camp showed that the tree was present in the region as early as the Neolithic (Dimbleby in Case 1956, 18), the only sub-sequent finds have been medieval.

GEOARCHAEOLOGICAL REPORT ON SOILS
Summary of report by M G Canti

A pinkish layer (1532) sealing a Roman pit near the northern edge of Area 9 (Pl. 9) was examined since it was thought possible that the layer had formed as the result of ploughing. However, the well-drained lime-stone soils which occur on the site are generally fully oxidised and so are unlikely to be chemically altered by agricultural activities. The pinkish layer is more likely to derive from an episode of levelling which exploited a patch of the pinkish clay which occurs naturally within the limestone gravels in the area of the site. As a result of earthworm burrowing the layer has grad-ually become mixed with the overlying darker topsoil.

Chapter 5: Scientific Evidence

RADIOCARBON DATES (Fig. 40)
Summary of report by Peter Marshall, Tim Allen, Tom Higham, J van der Plicht and R Sparks

Ten radiocarbon measurements were obtained on six samples from Spring Road Cemetery (Table 7). The samples were processed by the Oxford Radiocarbon Accelerator Unit in 2003 (Bronk Ramsey *et al.* forthcoming; Bronk Ramsey and Hedges 1997), the Centre for Isotope Research of the University of Groningen in 2003 (Aerts-Bijma *et al.* 1997 and 2001; van der Plicht *et al.* 2000), and the Rafter Radiocarbon Laboratory in 2002 (Bevan-Athfield and Sparks 2001; Zondervan and Sparks 1997). All three laboratories maintain continual programmes of quality assurance procedures, in addition to participation in international comparisons (Rozanski *et al.* 1992; Scott *et al.* 1988). These tests indicate no significant offsets and demonstrate the validity of the precision quoted. The stable isotope values ($\delta^{13}C$ and $\delta^{15}N$) are consistent with a very largely terrestrial diet, with only a minor component of marine protein although this is not likely to affect the radiocarbon dating (Chisholm *et al.* 1982; Mays 2000). The C:N ratios suggest that bone preservation was sufficiently good to have confidence in the radiocarbon determinations (Masters 1987; Tuross *et al.*1988).

The dates of Beaker skeleton 3036, which was associated with a possibly early copper awl, of the timber circle, and of three of the middle Iron Age skeletons (2199, 2125 and 2245) were established by radiocarbon determinations (Table 7; Fig. 40). The dates for the timber circle were obtained from a pig maxilla from a posthole (2328) in the inner arc and from a pig tibia in a posthole (2373) in the outer arc. The other dates were obtained on femurs from the skeletons involved.

The three measurements on the Beaker skeleton are statistically consistent and suggest that the burial dates from 2460–2200 cal BC (weighted mean).

The two measurements for the timber circle are not statistically consistent, but do suggest a middle Bronze Age date (1690–1510 cal BC and 1520–1310 cal BC).

The measurements for all of the Iron Age skeletons are statistically the same, indicating that they could all have been of the same age (400–230 cal BC, 400–205 cal BC and 410–260 cal BC). The 4th–3rd century cal BC date suggests that the early Iron Age pottery found in the graves was residual.

MAGNETOMETER AND MAGNETIC SUSCEPTIBILITY SURVEY
Summary of report by Alister Bartlett

The first stage of fieldwork consisted of magnetometer and magnetic susceptibility surveys of Blocks 5, 8 and 9 of the cemetery and the adjacent playing fields of Larkmead School (Figs 41 and 42). The plots of the magnetometer survey represent readings collected along lines spaced 1 m apart, using Geoscan fluxgate magnetometers. The x-y graphical plot (not illustrated) was corrected for irregularities in line spacing caused by variations in the instrument zero setting, and additional 2D low pass filtering has been applied to the grey scale plot (see Figure 41) to reduce background noise levels and emphasise the broader features, which may be archaeologically significant. In the magnetic susceptibility survey readings were taken at 10 m intervals using a Bartington MS2 meter and field sensor loop.

The survey suffered in many areas from disturbance by modern features, such as fences, benches, recent graves and buried iron, which obscured or were indistinguishable from archaeological features. In a few areas, however, more interesting results were achieved. In Areas 8 and 9 the north-south Roman ditches (A), pits (B), the Victorian quarry (E) and perhaps also the sunken-featured buildings (C and D) can be made out. In the southern playing field (Area B) one or two ditched enclosures and several pits were revealed.

Table 7 Radiocarbon dates.

Laboratory Number	Sample Number	Material & context	Radiocarbon Age (BP)	Weighted mean	Calibrated date range (68% confidence)	Calibrated date range (95% confidence)
OxA-12100 (note 1)	3036	Bone, human femur from skeleton 3036	3861±29			
NZA-15865	3036	Bone, human femur from skeleton 3036	3834±45			
NZA-15866	3036	Bone, human femur from skeleton 3036	3841±40	3850±21 T'=0.3; v=2; T'(5%)=6.0	2400–2210 cal BC	2460–2200 cal BC
OxA-12101 (note 2)	2125	Bone, human femur from skeleton 2125	2286±26		400–260 cal BC	400–230 cal BC
OxA-12102 (note 3)	2199	Bone, human femur from skeleton 2199	2253±27			
GrA-22752	2199	Bone, human femur from skeleton 2199	2310±50	2266±24 T'=1.0; v=1; T'(5%)=3.8	390–255 cal BC	400–205 cal BC
OxA-12103 (note 4)	2243	Bone, human femur from skeleton 2243	2301±27			
GrA-22754	2243	Bone, human femur from skeleton 2243	2330±60	2306±25 T'=0.2; v=1; T'(5%)=3.8	400–380 cal BC	410–260 cal BC
OxA-12376	2329	Bone, pig maxilla from posthole 2328	3294±30		1620–1520 cal BC	1690–1510 cal BC
OxA-12377	2375	Bone, pig tibia with gnaw marks from posthole 2373	3156±40		1500–1400 cal BC	1520–1310 cal BC

Notes:

1 Following the discovery of a technical problem with bone samples at the Oxford Radiocarbon Accelerator Unit in October 2002, the excess collagen from the original measurement on this sample was re-purified and re-dated. All the measurements are statistically consistent (OxA-12100; NZA-15865; NZA-15866 and OxA-X-2037-15 (3901±31BP), T'=2.2, T'(5%)=7.8, v=3; Ward and Wilson 1978). At the time of writing, the measurement of the re-purified collagen was still experimental, and so the re-date has not been included in the chronological model presented here.

2 The excess collagen from the original measurement on this sample was re-purified and re-dated. Both pairs of measurements are statistically consistent (OxA-12101 and OxA-X-2037-16 (2281±38BP), T'=0.0, T'(5%)=3.8, v=1; Ward and Wilson 1978).

3 The excess collagen from the original measurement on this sample was re-purified and re-dated. The experimental result is statistically inconsistent with the other measurements (OxA-12102; GrA-22752 and OxA-X-2037-17 (2357±26BP), T'=7.7, T'(5%)=6.0, v=2; Ward and Wilson 1978). This suggests that the re-ultrafiltration of the excess did not completely remove whatever contaminants affected the original measurement (in this particular case).

4 The excess collagen from the original measurement on this sample was re-purified and re-dated. All the measurements are statistically consistent (OxA-12103; GrA-22754 and OxA-X-2037-18 (2279±28BP), T'=0.7, T'(5%)=6.0, v=2; Ward and Wilson 1978).

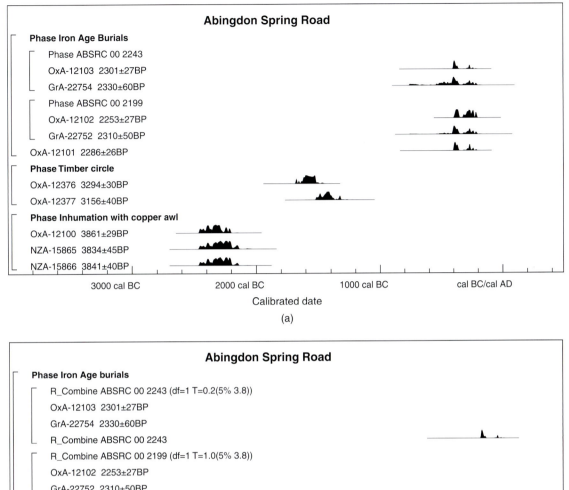

(a)

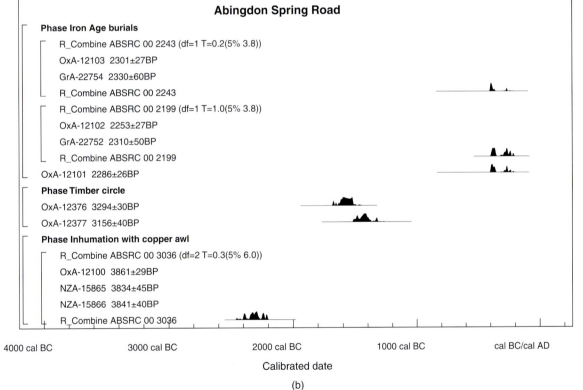

(b)

Figure 40   Radiocarbon dates: Probability distributions of dates from Abingdon Spring Road (a) before taking a weighted mean, and (b) after taking a weighted mean.

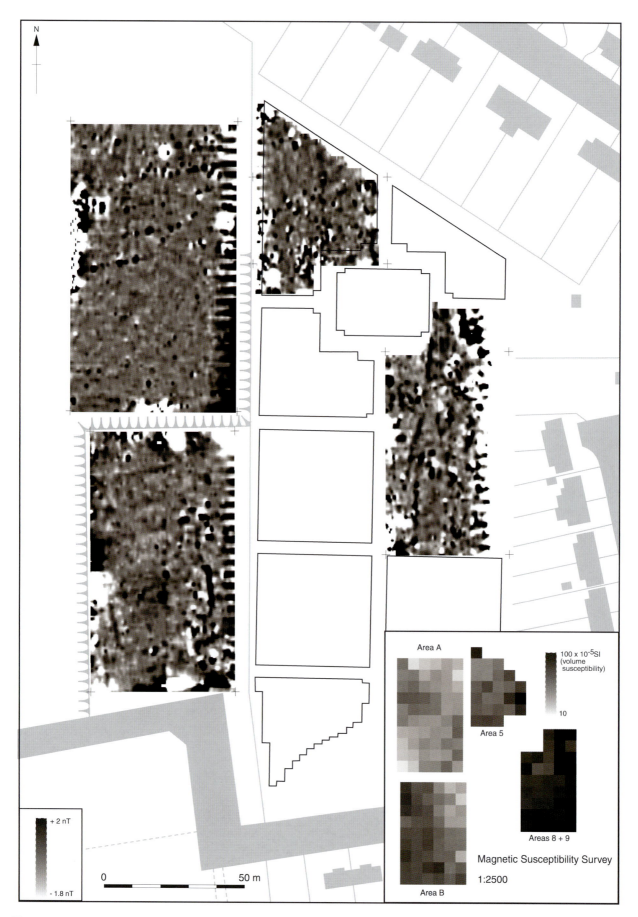

Figure 41 Magnetometer and magnetic susceptibility surveys of cemetery and area to the north west.

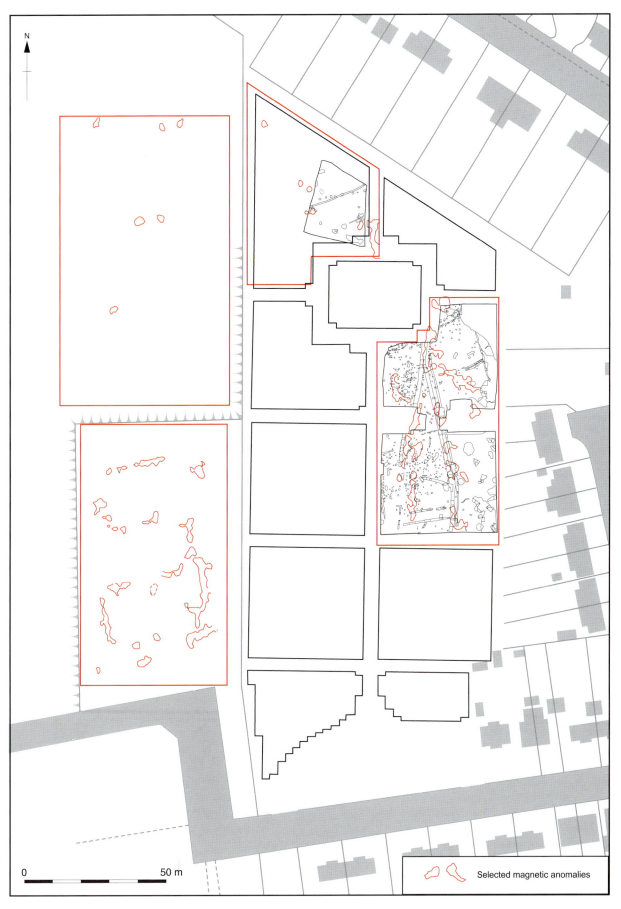

Figure 42   Magnetometer survey in relation to excavated features.

Chapter 6:   Discussion

by Tim Allen and Zena Kamash

INTRODUCTION

Artefacts recovered from the Spring Road Cemetery demonstrate human activity from the Mesolithic onwards. Most periods and phases of prehistory are represented by evidence of some sort, as is Roman and early Saxon occupation. This was evidently a favoured location for a variety of activities over a long period of time.

In the following discussion the nature of the archaeological investigations, and their scale, has to be borne in mind. The excavated areas were small, and covered only a quarter of the area of known finds. In addition, the find spots suggest that the site continued to the west towards the Larkhill Stream, an impression supported by local reports that archaeological material was seen when the playing fields were levelled, although no formal record of this was made. Although the geophysical survey confirms that any traces of archaeology were destroyed immediately west of the site during this levelling, traces of further ditches are indicated further north, perhaps indicating that the site continued in that direction. No investigation took place when the houses to the north and east were constructed, but a natural limit to the site to the north is provided by a branch of the Larkhill Stream, which flows down from the north-east some 250 m from the site. South of the site only a single small trench has been excavated (Ainslie 1999), and although this was sterile it is insufficient to rule out further archaeology in this direction. Overall, therefore, the excavations are not necessarily representative of all aspects of the past history of the site, and while indicative of the periods of activity represented, may not adequately characterise these activities.

Within the excavated part of the cemetery site levels taken on the surface of the natural gravel show that the gravel terrace was highest just east of the mid-line of the site at the north end of Area 8. There was a fall of over 1 m to the west and north-west between Areas 8 and 5, a distance of only 50 m, and the levels also show that the terrace was rising more gradually northwards, with a difference of 0.5 m over the 80 m from the south end of Area 9 to the north end of Area 8. On the east side of the site there appeared to be a corresponding drop in the level of gravel, but this may not have been natural, as this was the area riddled with medieval gravel pits, which may have resulted in a lowering of the overall level of the gravel. Nevertheless the northern end of the excavation area appears to have represented a high point in the local topography.

MESOLITHIC PERIOD
by Tim Allen

In the local area Mesolithic sites are common along the banks of the Thames, presumably reflecting the presence of openings in the tree cover at the riverside and the greater ease of movement by water in this landscape. These sites include Thrupp (Wallis 1981), Abingdon Vineyard (P Bradley in prep.), Andersey Island (Ainslie 1991) and Corporation Farm, Drayton (Shand *et al.* 2003). Major tributaries such as the Ock are also likely to have been used in this way. Even if not navigable, lesser watercourses such as the Larkhill Stream may also have provided easier pathways to travel on foot, and will certainly have been reference points in the landscape. Small collections of Mesolithic flint have been found on the west bank of the Larkhill stream at Ashville (Skellington in Parrington 1978, 90) and Wyndyke Furlong (Bradley in Muir and Roberts 1999, 40–42), as well as at Spring Road on the east side. Ethnographic studies of modern hunter-gatherers shows that a single community may have ranged over a territory as much as 20 miles across, and will have included hilltop sites like those on Boars Hill overlooking the Thames at Oxford some 4 miles to the north (Allen 1993b; Holgate 1986).

The nature of the archaeological investigations, and the small numbers of struck flints recovered (Chapter 3), make it impossible to be sure what sort of activities were being carried out during the Mesolithic. The small numbers of struck flints may indicate that this was merely a stop-off point during a hunting trip, though it is also possible that activity was on a larger scale, but was focussed outside the areas investigated. Access to water will have been important both for people and the animals they hunted, and locations such as this close to streams will therefore have been suitable for occupation.

NEOLITHIC ACTIVITY
by Zena Kamash and Tim Allen

Neolithic activity at Spring Road includes material of every major pottery tradition. There is a limited number of sherds of early Neolithic Plain Bowl pottery, much of a Peterborough Ware dish and a pit containing Grooved Ware (see Chapter 3). The Bronze Age timber circle contained residual sherds of all these traditions. Another possible Neolithic feature may have been disturbed during modern grave-digging (3506, 4 D 26). Finds from this grave included 31 flints (probably mid to late Neolithic in date) and 9 animal bones in very good condition. Spatial analysis of the finds distribution shows that

Neolithic activity was confined to the northern part of the site (Areas 4 and 8), corresponding to the highest ground.

Early Neolithic

For the early Neolithic the evidence is limited to a few sherds of Plain Bowl pottery, all residual in later contexts. None of the struck flint is diagnostically early Neolithic. The surrounding area was clearly a significant focus for early Neolithic people, as it contained a causewayed enclosure at Radley (Barclay and Halpin 1999), a cursus and mortuary enclosure at Drayton (Barclay *et al.* 2003) and possibly an earthen long mound by the Ock just 1.5 km southwest of the site at Tesco (OAU 1997; see Fig. 43). Away from the monuments domestic sites are mostly known from lithic finds or scatters (Holgate 1986; Holgate 1988), though Plain Bowl pottery was found at Corporation Farm south of the Ock (Shand *et al.* 2003). The discovery of Plain Bowl pottery at Spring Road is therefore significant. The relatively small-scale nature of most sites in the Upper Thames Valley, and the limited evidence for arable agriculture, suggests that these early farming communities were still fairly mobile, moving frequently within local territories. This may therefore have been a short-lived occupation site.

Middle Neolithic

A semi-complete Peterborough Ware dish was discovered during modern grave-digging, and its good condition would suggest that it came from a cut feature (Chapter 3). A sherd from a second vessel was also found in the Bronze Age posthole arc. A possibly middle Neolithic pit may have been disturbed during modern grave-digging (3506, 4 D 26).

The middle Neolithic activity associated with Peterborough Ware at Spring Road takes place within the same monumental context as in the early Neolithic. These ceramic finds belong to the same period as those recovered from the later use of the causewayed enclosure at Radley, adjacent to which earthen long mounds were constructed in this period (Avery 1982; Cleal 1999). Peterborough Ware is also associated with the cursus at Drayton and the ditches of the probable long barrow at Tesco (OAU 1997), showing that all of these monument complexes remained active. The only other non-monumental site of the period on the west side of Abingdon is at Corporation Farm south of the Ock, where (as at Spring Road) the site has produced both early Neolithic Plain Bowl pottery and Peterborough Ware (Shand *et al.* 2003).

Late Neolithic

Grooved Ware pit 2622

This pit had escaped destruction by the later medieval gravel-extraction pits in the south-eastern corner of Area 8. As is typical with such pits, it was a relatively shallow bowl-shaped pit that contained a variety of finds in a matrix of burnt material (Thomas 1999, 74). Pits of this shape are considered to be unsuitable for the storage of foodstuffs, in contrast to the deeper, straight-sided and flat-bottomed pits of the Iron Age period (Reynolds 1974, 126–7; Thomas 1999, 64). The construction of the deposits in the Spring Road pit point to different interpretations for the function of these pits.

The distribution of finds retrieved from pit fills 2620 and 2619 also displays some very interesting patterns (summarized in Table 8) with the range of material in 2620 being seemingly more selective than that in 2619. As noted by Lamdin-Whymark ('Detailed report', Chapter 3), the struck flint shows signs of structured deposition, the lower fill (2620) containing a single core and seven retouched tools while 2619 contained two cores, a tested nodule and only one retouched artefact. In addition, a higher proportion of the flint was burnt in the lower than in the higher deposit: 15% in 2620 and 4.5% in 2619.

The distribution of animal bone, which was well-preserved, also shows significant variation. Of the 24 identified bones in 2620 (including sieved material), 20 were pig of which 18 were head elements and 2 were foot elements. Three cattle ribs and one sheep phalanx were also retrieved. In deposit 2619, however, out of the 27 identified bones (including sieved material), 11 were pig, 8 were sheep, 5 were cattle and 3 were pine marten. In addition, there was no clear preference for head over other elements: 32% head, 36% ribs and 32% other. Furthermore, while none of the bones from 2620 had been butchered, 3 of the identified bones from 2619 showed signs of butchery, although the condition of the bones was slightly worse in 2619. Table 8 also indicates that the condition of the pottery and fired clay was slightly better in 2620 than in 2619, as in both cases the average weight was higher. In addition, 2619 contained two small residual sherds of Plain Bowl pottery.

The flint assemblage provides some clues for the interpretation of these deposits. Although a high proportion of the flint was used and in some cases broken during use, the cores found in the pit, including those in 2619, were all large with no obvious faults or knapping errors and had not been exhausted (Chapter 3). In contrast, 2620 contained an end and side scraper (SF 44) that had been snapped rendering it useless. The pit therefore included specially-selected items, including both items that were still useful and those that had been deliberately rendered useless or 'killed'. Furthermore, no refits were found in the assemblage, despite there being groups of flakes whose raw material strongly suggested that they had come from the same cores (Chapter 3). This shows that some of the flakes from these cores had not been deposited in the pit, although manufactured during the same knapping process.

The exclusion of some flake material from the pit raises the possibility that all of the material in the pit had been specifically selected for deposition. One

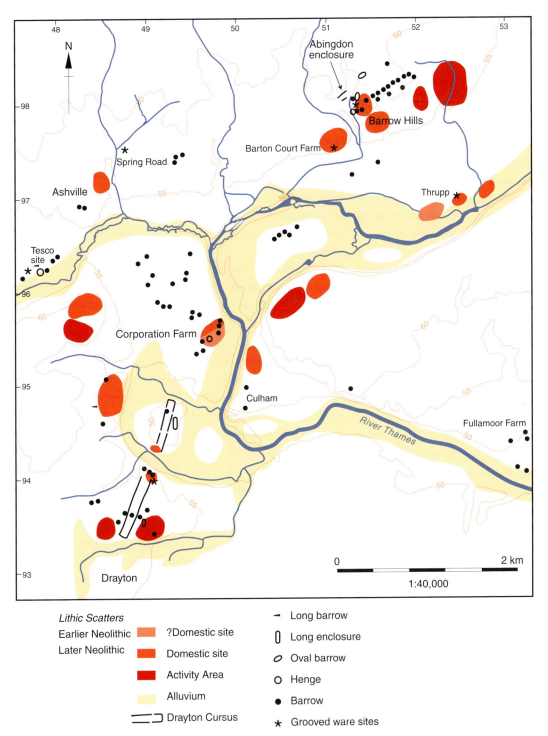

Figure 43   Spring Road in relation to Neolithic and Early Bronze Age monuments around Abingdon.

possibility is that the selected material was intended to be representative of the activities carried out on this visit to the site, rather than all of the refuse generated from them. In this case the cores could represent tool production, the domestic animal bones feasting, the marten and hazel nuts hunting and gathering, and so on. Thus, this pit and its contents were made into a 'durable trace' of an event such as a feast, gathering or period of occupation

and even the digging of the pit became an event in and for itself (Thomas 1999, 70 and 73).

The pit fills add support to the idea that this pit may have been filled as one event. The pit contained only a small deposit of primary gravel slumping before being largely filled with two dark, charcoal-rich and homogeneous deposits, whose homogeneous nature suggests that the pit was filled quickly (*cf.* Thomas 1999, 64). The last fill was a thin layer in the very top, probably plough-disturbed. In addition, the sides of the pit were steep with no evidence of weathering at the top. Furthermore, the fresh condition of the finds (with the possible exception of the pottery) indicate that the activities or events from which they derived occurred only shortly before the digging and filling of the pit. The flint was in remarkably good condition and very fresh (Chapter 3). The animal bone was also in very good condition, 98.5% of the assemblage (excluding sieved material) being classed as Grade 1 or 2 (Lyman 1996, where Grade 1 is the best-preserved and Grade 5 the worst-preserved bone). Furthermore, none of the animal bone showed signs of gnawing, indicating that it had not been left exposed to scavenging by dogs. This indicates, therefore, that the material in the pit was not subject to provisional discard nor deposited first in another location such as a midden.

Pit-digging reached a zenith at the end of the Neolithic with pits associated with Grooved Ware (Thomas 1999, 69 and fig. 4.4) and such pits are also known from the Abingdon area (Fig. 43). The Grooved Ware from Spring Road included not only the Woodlands style vessels from the pit but also a sherd of Durrington Walls style. Among the other pits in the Abingdon Area those containing Woodlands style pottery include one from Corporation Farm only 2 km to the south (Shand *et al.* 2003), two from Sutton Courtenay some 5 km to the south (Leeds 1934) and several from the area around the Abingdon causewayed enclosure at Daisy Banks *c* 4 km to the east. (Barclay and Halpin 1999). In addition, Durrington Walls style Grooved Ware vessels have been found in a pit beneath the A34 2 km south-west of Spring Road (Balkwill in Parrington 1978, figs 28–9) and in pits at Barton Court Farm (Miles 1986, fig. 4) some 3 km to the east (see also Barclay 1999, figs 2.1–3). Further Grooved Ware pits have been found at Cassington (Case 1982) and a Neolithic pit (no further details) was also found across the Larkhill Stream south of Ashville during redevelopment (Chambers 1986).

There are some finds common to most of these pits: almost all contain charred hazelnuts, and as at Spring Road pig bones predominate at Barton Court and at Radley, Barrow Hills (Robinson in Barclay and Halpin 1999, 271). The occurrence of other materials such as cereals, wild animal bones, worked bones or axe fragments is, however, much more variable, and may indicate the process of deliberate selection at work; a correlation has recently been suggested between the range of finds present and the fineness and decoration of the pottery (Barclay 1999, 14–15). Taken at face value the finds from Spring Road would suggest a largely pastoral economy supplemented by hunting and gathering, but since the finds were probably selected for deposition, they may reflect only materials deemed appropriate for deposition in pits (that is a ritual assemblage), and may not be representative of the full range of farming practices of the users of Grooved Ware.

An open cleared landscape would fit with the environmental evidence from Radley, Barrow Hills east of Abingdon (Robinson 1999, 271–2). Nevertheless, the contents of the pit at Spring Road suggest that there was woodland in the vicinity, with hazelnuts in the pit and coniferous woodland indicated by the pine marten bones. Some arable is also indicated by charred wheat grains, and domestic livestock included pig, sheep and cattle.

The evidence of the pit below the A34 and those at Barrow Hills suggests that the monuments of the early and middle Neolithic continued to be visited in the late Neolithic. Within this period new monuments were also added. No major henge monuments like those at Dorchester-on-Thames (Whittle *et al.* 1992, 184–93) or Stanton Harcourt (Barclay *et al.* 1995) are known at Abingdon, but a small Class 2 henge monument was constructed at Corporation Farm (Abingdon and District Arch. Soc. 1973; Shand *et al.* 2003; see also Fig. 43). Balkwill argued that a crop-mark ring ditch with an apparent gap on the north just south of Tesco (and only 1.5 km from Spring Road) was a Class 1 henge. A trench has since been dug

Table 8   Summary of contents of Grooved Ware pit 2622.

Material	2621	2620	2619	2623	Total	Comments
Grooved Ware		3 (16 g)	2 (2 g)		5 (18 g)	2 vessels represented in 2620
Plain Bowl			2 (4 g)		2 (4 g)	Residual sherds
Fired Clay		12 (168 g)	3 (35 g)		15 (203 g)	Probably structural clay
Flint		95	124	2	221	Some deliberately snapped pieces, including a scraper High proportion of retouch and burning
Animal bone (bulk)	1	62	132	1	196	75.8% (2620) and 81% (2619) were unidentifiable
Animal bone (sieved)		216	47		264	Almost 96% unidentifiable material
Hazelnut(s)		5	5		10	
Cereal		1	1		2	*Triticum* sp. plausibly Neolithic, but possibly later contamination?
Charcoal						Some oak, hazel, *pomoideae* indet

across the south side (OAU 1997), and a Beaker sherd and struck flint were found in the topmost fill, so this remains a possibility (Balkwill in Parrington 1978, 29).

BEAKER PERIOD
by Tim Allen

Beaker period activity is evident at Spring Road both from the grave accompanied by a copper awl in Area 5, from a sherd within a small pit or posthole in Area 8 and from other sherds of pottery and struck flints found by earlier grave-digging further south. The grave is of considerable interest, as it is radiocarbon-dated between 2460 and 2200 cal BC, making the burial very early in the Beaker period, and the copper awl accompanying the body one of the earliest copper objects from Britain. The pottery sherds from elsewhere on the site are also decorated with styles that place them early in the Beaker period, before 2000 BC (Chapter 3).

Locally early radiocarbon dates have also been obtained from two burials with copper objects at Radley, Barrow Hills (dating to 2700–2100 and 2650–2000 respectively), and together with the burial from Yarnton that was accompanied by a copper bar neck ring (Clarke *et al.* 1985, 270–2), this points to an early focus of metal-using activity in this part of the Upper Thames Valley. The burial at Spring Road, which is more closely dated than those from Barrow Hills, adds a fourth to this group, and considerably strengthens the case for an early Beaker focus in this area. Another relatively early date (2330–1950 cal BC) was obtained for the Radley burial with a double-tanged awl, though this was of tin-bronze (Northover in Barclay and Halpin 1999, 192–5).

It has been suggested (Garwood 1999) that Woodlands-style pottery indicates a later 3rd millennium date. This makes the relationship between the Grooved Ware pit at Spring Road and the early Beaker burial of particular interest. Given the close physical proximity of the pit and grave at Spring Road, the location of the burial may not have been coincidental, but at the least may have made use of a site with ancestral links, and it is even possible that the events were contemporary.

There is growing evidence in the area of late Grooved Ware activity as well as of the early use of copper. Woodlands pottery with later 3rd millennium dates comes from two Grooved Ware features at Radley (Barclay and Halpin 1999). Grooved Ware with comb-decoration has been found locally at Yarnton, the latter a style of decoration normally associated with Beaker pottery (Barclay and Edwards in prep.). In this context it is unfortunate that radiocarbon-dating of the Grooved Ware pit at Spring Road was not carried out as part of the English Heritage programme.

The burial at Spring Road is female, and is accompanied solely by the copper awl. This awl is of the double-tanged type usually associated with Beaker burials. Clarke (1970) and Gibbs (1989) demonstrated a strong association between female

burials and awls. The orientation of the burial, lying on its right side and with the head to the SSE, is a common one for female burials of this date in the region; there are three comparable examples of adult female Beaker burials in the Stanton Harcourt complex (Barclay *et al.* 1995, 80–81, 99–100 and 105), and a fourth unsexed adult in the same position as well (ibid., 88). There are only four adult females of the late Neolithic and early Bronze Age in the group from Radley, but of these, two early Bronze Age examples are laid on the right side with their heads to the south (Barclay and Halpin 1999, 120–126).

The Beaker burial at Spring Road appears to be a 'flat' grave without any associated monument. There is a tradition of Beaker 'flat' graves in the Upper Thames Valley, with more 'flat' burials than burials within ditched barrows both at Radley and at Stanton Harcourt (Barclay and Halpin 1999, 324). There are other examples locally from Yarnton (Hey in prep.). Those at Radley can perhaps be seen as loosely associated with the burial monuments, all comprising a cemetery area, but some of those at Yarnton do not have any clear links to monuments. Barclay argued that the close spacing of two at Radley, and their lack of secondary deposits, suggested that they had never been covered by large mounds, perhaps only by mounds large enough to cover the area of the grave cut. These burials sometimes occur in groups or 'cemeteries'; there were at least four at Radley, and it is therefore possible that some of the other crouched burials found at the Spring Road cemetery may have been of this date. The other fragments of Beaker recovered from the site may have derived either from funerary or domestic contexts.

Beaker sherds, some fingernail-impressed, one cord-impressed, were also recovered from Wyndyke Furlong just across the Larkhill Stream. Barclay argued for a separation of burial and pit deposits, citing Wyndyke Furlong as an example of domestic activity on the low terraces or floodplain (Barclay *et al.* 1999, 324), but this burial at Spring Road is less than 300 m distant. If the activity at these two sites was contemporary, then it would indicate that pits and burials do occur in relatively close proximity. The Beaker activity at Wyndyke Furlong has not however been radiocarbon-dated, and may be later than that at Spring Road.

Beaker activity is also known 1.5 km to the southwest, where a group of ring ditches is clustered around the long barrow at the Tesco site just north of the river Ock. Evaluation at this site recovered a Beaker sherd from one of the ring ditches, and parts of two domestic Beaker vessels from a small pit south of the ring-ditches (OAU 1997). The pottery appears to be later than that at Spring Road, the decorative styles usually dated after 2000 BC. Sherds of a 'southern Beaker' were found in East St Helen's Street in central Abingdon, and residual sherds in the Vineyard (Wilson and Wallis 1991, 4; Barclay pers. comm.).

The number of locations around Abingdon that have produced Beaker pottery is greater than that producing Grooved Ware, perhaps indicating the spread of clearance and an increase in population.

BRONZE AGE
by Tim Allen and Zena Kamash

Early Bronze Age

Early Bronze Age activity at Spring Road is attested by a small group of decorated sherds recovered from modern graves, and by a single sherd possibly also of this date recovered from a shallow posthole in Area 9. No cremated remains were apparently associated with these finds, although the early Bronze Age pottery is interpreted as belonging to a ritual or funerary vessel (Chapter 3). At this period burials are normally associated with monuments, of which (as in the Beaker period) there is no evidence on this site. However, if it was a ritual or funerary vessel, it lay less than 300 m from two ring-ditches of this period at Ashville to the south-west across the Larkhill Stream (Balkwill in Parrington 1978, 25–30). An alternative possibility is that the vessel was in fact domestic; evidence for the occurrence of Collared Urn pottery in a probable domestic context has recently been found in a pit group at Taplow Court, Buckinghamshire (Allen and Lambdin-Whymark 2004).

The pattern of ring-ditches west of Abingdon at this period partly demonstrates the continued use of the sites of ancient monuments; there are ring ditches grouped around the long barrows at Tesco, adjacent to the Drayton cursus, and around the henge monument at Corporation Farm (Fig. 43). However, there are other burial sites that appear to be new, such as three barrows known from cropmarks in Barrow Field 400 m east of Spring Road, the two at Ashville and those at Saxton Road south of the Ock, part of a large cemetery group spreading south and east to Corporation Farm (Fig. 43). Unlike Radley, Barrow Hills, where burial was concentrated in one large linear cemetery, the pattern on the west side of Abingdon appears to have been more dispersed; whether Radley, Barrow Hills, was restricted to a particular wealthy social group, to which the barrows west of Abingdon were complementary, or whether these were different social groups using distinct burial sites, is unclear. If the latter is true, it would perhaps suggest that the social organisation west of Abingdon was more fragmented, with more independent social groups each creating its own local burial site.

Snails from the ring-ditches at Ashville showed that the barrows were situated in an open grassland environment (Robinson and Wilson 1987, 38). The number of barrow sites of the Beaker/early Bronze Age, even if not all contemporary, indicate numerous pockets of open or cleared ground around Abingdon, close enough to one another to suggest extensive areas of open grassland by the end of the period. Details of the diversity of the local Beaker/early Bronze Age environment are little clearer than those

of the late Neolithic, but clues are provided by the barley and wheat grains, and the acorns, found in a pit south of Tesco (OA 1997). The general picture in this period is provided by a pollen sequence at Daisy Banks Fen near to the barrow cemetery at Radley (Parker 1999), which shows an open landscape continuing from the late Neolithic to the end of the early Bronze Age (see also Robinson 1999, 272–3).

Middle Bronze Age

The timber circle

In Area 8 in the 2000 excavations a double arc of postholes was revealed. Only part of this monument lay within the excavation, and this limits the confidence with which questions about its form, function and associations can be addressed.

The Spring Road structure is assumed to have been circular in shape and perhaps 18–20 m in diameter. The arc that lay within the excavation appears to represent slightly less than quarter of a circle, though given the slightly irregular line of the postholes it is not possible to be certain. If the monument was circular, a limit of less than 32 m in diameter is provided by the excavation in Area 5, where no trace of the monument was found. It is possible that the arc was part of a much larger structure of different shape, but since no trace of it was found either in the NW corner of Area 8 or in evaluation trench F, this seems less likely.

The double arc of postholes is interpreted as belonging to a timber circle rather than a roundhouse because the diameter of the structure is very large for a roundhouse, and the outer arc of posts contains the larger posts, unlike the double-ring large roundhouses of the 1st millennium BC. The postholes of the outer arc are also very close together, unlike those of most houses, and must have formed almost a continuous palisade. Timber circles are normally Neolithic in date, but the radiocarbon dates of 3294±30 BP for a pig bone from posthole 2328 in the inner arc, and 3156±40 BP for bone from posthole 2373 in the outer arc, indicate a middle Bronze Age date, making this a very late example of such monuments. Similar reliable radiocarbon dates have been retrieved from timber circles at Navan B, Co. Armagh (3140±90 BP) and Poole, Dorset (3210±50 BP); later radiocarbon dates have also been retrieved from Haughey's Fort, Ireland and Ogden Down, Wiltshire (Gibson 1998, 48 fig. 39). It is noteworthy that both of these later examples were double circles (Gibson 1998, 59), which shows that there are later prehistoric parallels for the postulated inner ring of posts at Spring Road, even though at Ogden Down it was the inner ring of posts that was more substantial (Green 2000, 115–6).

The lack of any encircling ditch at Spring Road is paralleled at a number of other timber circles. Within the Upper Thames Valley other excavated examples without ditches include the late Neolithic Sites III–VI at Dorchester-on-Thames (Gibson 1998, 126–7), the penannular post circle at Gravelly Guy, Oxon. (Barclay *et al.* 1995, 88) and (possibly) the post circle at Langford Downs, Oxon. (Williams 1946–7; see also below). Of the Dorchester group only Site 3 at 20 m by 17 m was of similar size to that at Spring Road (Whittle *et al.* 1992, 169–175). The post-circle at Gravelly Guy, which predated the Iron Age settlement there but is otherwise undated, had a similar diameter of 18.75 m (Fig. 44); that at Langford Downs, which is also undated, was slightly smaller at 16 m in diameter. Although the excavator interpreted the latter site as late Iron Age on general spatial grounds, it has since been suggested that it might have been earlier (Healy 2004). If so, the presence of late Bronze Age/early Iron Age residual pottery on the site might indicate a later prehistoric date. There is also a cropmark circle of pits or postholes recently identified at Eynsham (Gibson 1998, 29 fig. 20), and another at Radley only 3 km from Spring Road (Gibson pers. comm.), though both of these may be late Neolithic rather than Bronze Age.

The timber circle at Spring Road stands out from these other examples because the distance between the posts is very small, indicating an almost continuous palisade. There was a long tradition of later Neolithic palisades at sites such as Mount Pleasant, Dorset, and West Kennet, Wilts (Whittle 1997). Some of the circles at Dorchester-on-Thames also had closely-spaced posts. For the Bronze Age, the spacing of the posts is most comparable to Seahenge, Holme, Norfolk, where the ring of posts has been described as a 'wall of wood' (Pryor 2001, 246). The size of the Seahenge circle is however much smaller, and the posts were apparently set within a continuous trench (see Fig. 44).

Another Upper Thames late Bronze Age post-circle at Standlake, Oxon, surrounded a ring-ditch (Gibson 1998, 59; Catling 1982, 97; see also Fig. 44). This is also the case at Ogden Down, and Green's reconstructions of this arrangement include one roofing the barrow (Green 2000, fig. 84). From the proportion of the Spring Road circle excavated it is unlikely that this surrounded a ring-ditch, though a central feature such as a burial, or a tree like that at Seahenge is still possible.

Only one or two of the postholes in the arc showed any sign of replacement, and it is therefore possible that the structure was only in use for a relatively short time. Brück (1999, 146–149) has argued that many middle Bronze Age structures had only a single-generation life-span. While the lifespan of timbers such as these in the local soils is hard to judge, the timber circle may have lasted for only 30–100 years.

The timber circle at Spring Road was not seen by the excavators until a layer very similar to the Holocene subsoil (layer 2648) was removed, revealing an arc of posts cut into the natural gravel. This layer (2648) was so similar to the subsoil that it was not recorded consistently, but appears to have sealed the majority of the postholes in the post arc(s). The fact that this layer directly overlay the gravel indicates either that the original Holocene topsoil had been stripped before the structure was built, or that

this was a ploughsoil that truncated the structure. This layer must have been deposited between the middle Bronze Age, during which the postholes were infilled, and the middle Iron Age, when a posthole was cut through this layer. It is likely to have formed some time after the timber circle went out of use, as the majority of the postholes have a thin deposit of friable dark greyish-brown clayey silt in their tops, also sealed by 2648, that appears to have been deposited in the hollows left after the postholes, including those with post pipes, no longer held posts.

Layer 2648 was confined to the north-eastern sector of Area 8, and did not spread much further south than the southernmost postholes of the outer arc. It is possible that this layer was derived from a mound within, and possibly even revetted by, the timber circle. In this case, the topsoil would have to have been stripped before the monument was constructed. In Britain timber circles of stakes are sometimes found under barrows, for instance at Buckskin Barrow, Basingstoke (Allen, M, *et al.* 1995), but are only rarely contemporary parts of the barrow structure. One such example was at Barnack, Cambridgeshire (Donaldson 1977), where there was a double circle. The circles at this site however consisted of stakeholes, not postholes, and such structures are generally much slighter than the structure implied by the posts of the Spring Road circle. Furthermore, there was no surrounding ditch such as is usual with barrows.

Palisaded barrows without surrounding ditches are however a recognised type in the Netherlands, as at Wessinghuizen, where a double palisade encircled a turf mound (Gibson 1998, 72). The fact that layer 2648 did not slump into the tops of the postholes however inclines towards interpretation as a plough-soil rather than slip from a mound.

Reconstruction of this structure is uncertain. Mercer (1981) suggested that the height of the posts above ground could be calculated using a ratio of 3:1 or 3.5: 1 in relation to the original depth of the posthole. More recently Gibson has revisited these figures, and suggested that a ratio of 4:1 is commonly used in practice today (Gibson 1998, 106–7). Using the 3.5: 1 ratio as a compromise, the posts would have been a minimum of 1.57–2.31 m high. If the sealing layer was a ploughsoil, then the postholes are likely to have been at least 0.1 m deeper, and the posts at least 0.3 m longer (ie 1.87–2.61 m high), preventing a view of the interior. If not, the posts would have stood c 1.12–1.68 m above the ground, significantly lower than the 3 m calculated for Seahenge (Pryor 2001, 270), but adequate for a revetment (see reconstructions page 8 and 66).

On balance, the structure is more likely to have been a freestanding timber circle than a barrow. Its location corresponds to the highest part of the site, presumably to increase both the visual impressiveness of the monument as it was approached, and to make it more visible in the surrounding landscape. It is also possible that the siting of the monument was

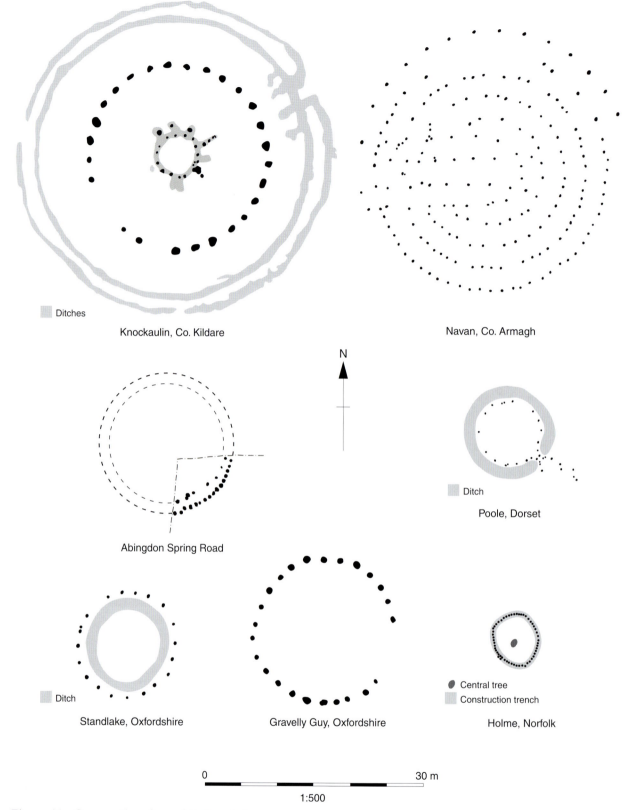

Ditches

Knockaulin, Co. Kildare

Navan, Co. Armagh

N

Abingdon Spring Road

Ditch

Poole, Dorset

Ditch

Standlake, Oxfordshire

Gravelly Guy, Oxfordshire

● Central tree

Construction trench

Holme, Norfolk

0   30 m

1:500

Figure 44   Comparative plans of timber circles.

influenced by the previous history of burial and deposition in this location, though direct evidence for continuity over the 600–700 years between the Beaker burial and this structure is slight.

The function of the timber circle is hard to define, particularly as only a quarter of the structure itself, and less than half of its immediate surroundings, have been excavated. It is generally considered that while such structures did play an important part in rituals and ceremonies, these did not involve feasting (Gibson 1998, 82), and the lack of associated artefactual evidence at Spring Road perhaps supports this. After 2000 BC timber circles tend to become increasingly focussed on burials (Gibson 1998, 58). No certain middle Bronze Age burials were found in association with the part of the Spring Road circle that was excavated. A pit containing the base of a large middle Bronze Age pot was found in Area 9 some 40 m south of the timber arc. This shallow pit appeared to have been severely truncated, but also contained sherds from a second Bucket Urn. The absence of any cremated material at all, when a little of the side of the vessel was present, may well indicate that this was not a cremation urn. A group of pits containing large middle Bronze Age vessels, some set into pits in the ground, have however recently been found in the Middle Thames Valley at Cippenham (Ford *et al.* 2003, 39–40 and 71–77), and of these pits some contained very small quantities of cremated bone. These pits and pots were therefore interpreted as deliberate deposits associated with funerary rites, even if not cremation containers themselves. Middle Bronze Age cremation burials were found in a barrow only 300 m to the south-west of the Spring Road site, across the Larkhill Stream at Ashville (Parrington 1978), so even if the vessel at Spring Road was not funerary, a loose association with burial is possible.

More practical functions should not however be excluded. Fenced rings this sort of size are still used today for breaking and training horses, and evidence for horse-riding in Britain starts in the middle Bronze Age. There is however no direct evidence to support this suggestion. Such a use would not exclude a ritual function, as religious and secular activities are unlikely to have been divorced from one another in British prehistory.

Whatever the precise function of this timber structure, its very existence is significant. Only a handful of middle or late Bronze Age examples have yet been discovered in Britain, and these exhibit considerable variety in form and associations, as discussed above. While stone and timber circles are an important and common element of the late Neolithic and Beaker periods, their role in the belief system of the middle and late Bronze Age is rarely mentioned. There is of course no reason why stone circles should not have continued as ritual foci throughout the Bronze Age and beyond, but in areas where stone was uncommon, such as the Upper Thames Valley, few such monuments were apparently constructed (only the Devil's Quoits at Stanton Harcourt), and wooden structures would have needed repeated repair, or rebuilding. On current evidence the Upper Thames Valley, compared to the rest of the country, appears to contain a concentration of these, perhaps indicating a shared regional belief system or cultural identity. At present the rarity of timber circles of this date makes this site, and its location, likely to have been a matter of

especial significance. As this site is however small and archaeologically inconspicuous, the possibility must be borne in mind that many more such sites remain to be discovered.

Other features containing only Bronze Age pottery, which comprise two short lengths of gully and six postholes, may all contain residual material and be later in date; similar gullies were however found at Wyndyke Furlong predating the main Iron Age occupation, and were tentatively dated to the Bronze Age (Muir and Roberts 1999, 13 fig. 2.8). It is therefore possible that there was a spread of later Bronze Age activity along both sides of the Larkhill Stream. The Spring Road site, like the waterhole at Tesco and Eight-Acre Field, shows evidence of both middle and late Bronze Age activity, implying some continuity of use in the later Bronze Age.

The context of the middle Bronze Age activity

Twenty years ago there was little settlement evidence of the middle or late Bronze Age in this area (Bradley 1986). Since then the number and variety of sites of these periods has increased enormously (Fig. 45). Around Abingdon itself there were settlement enclosures at Corporation Farm, burials around one of the ring-ditches at Ashville, a waterhole and other features adjacent to the ring-ditches at Tesco and linear ditches and settlement traces at Wyndyke Furlong (OAU 1997, 5; Muir and Roberts 1999). East of Abingdon there is a further settlement at Eight Acre Field, Radley (Mudd 1995), and middle Bronze Age burials are found around the earlier barrows at Radley, Barrow Hills (Barclay *et al.* 1999).

Excavations at Yarnton have demonstrated that the floodplain of the Thames was a favoured location for settlement in the early and middle Bronze Age, with a number of roundhouses being found. The enclosures at Corporation Farm lie close to the gravel terrace edge, and it is also possible that the main focus of settlement along the river Ock lay close to the river on the floodplain at sites such as that next to Tesco, some way south of the Spring Road site.

Beyond the immediate neighbourhood of the site, enclosure and field systems have been investigated at Fullamoor Farm, Clifton Hampden (Booth *et al.* 1993), Appleford Sidings (Booth and Simmonds in prep.), Mount Farm and Berinsfield (Lambrick 1992, 89, fig. 29), and have been identified from cropmarks at Northfield Farm, Long Wittenham (Miles 1977; Baker 2002). They have also been found further west between Steventon and East Hannay (Hearne 2000). A Deverel-Rimbury cemetery has been found at Long Wittenham (Leeds 1929; Case *et al.* 1964, figs 28 and 29; Bradley 1986, 42). Large ditched enclosures of defensive proportions have recently been investigated at Castle Hill, Little Wittenham (Allen and Lamdin-Whymark 2005) and at Eynsham (Barclay *et al.* 2001), while metalwork has been dredged from the Thames at Days' Lock, Dorchester, Culham Reach and Sandford-on-Thames (York 2002). Not all of these sites are contemporary, but

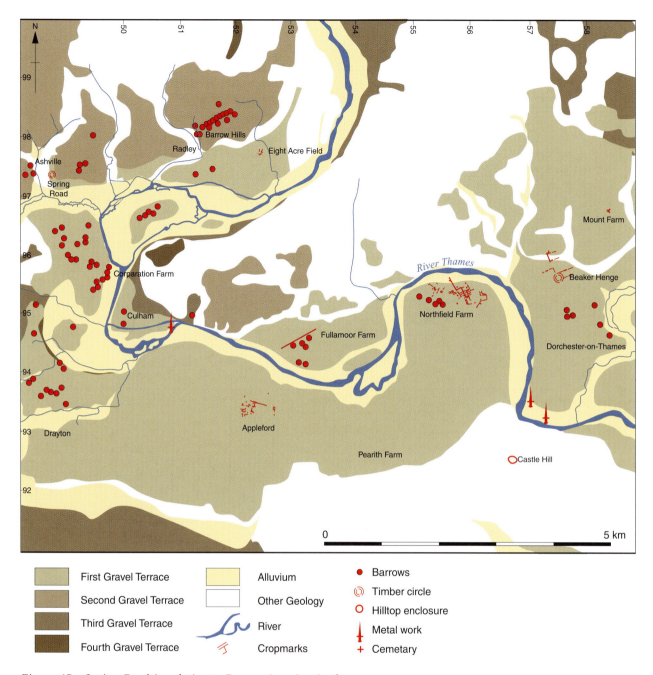

Figure 45 Spring Road in relation to Bronze Age sites in the area.

they clearly indicate settlement of considerable scale and complexity in this part of the Upper Thames Valley in the middle to late Bronze Age (Fig. 45), to which the timber circle at Spring Road adds a further dimension.

Environmental evidence from the site for the middle and late Bronze Age is limited. The layer that overlay the postholes of the timber circle has been interpreted as accumulating either in the late Bronze Age or early Iron Age, and as either a ploughsoil or a newly formed topsoil. If it was the latter, it would presumably have formed in the centuries following the abandonment of the timber circle, most likely in the late Bronze Age. If a ploughsoil, a context in the

late Bronze Age would also seem more likely than the early Iron Age, when there was a timber building immediately adjacent, and possibly a penannular enclosure as well. Pollen evidence from the wider catchment for this period is lacking, as there is an hiatus in accumulation at Daisy Bank Fen after the early Bronze Age (Parker 1999).

IRON AGE
by Tim Allen

At Spring Road Iron Age activity is of several kinds, including a circular roundhouse of several possible phases, other postholes, several crouched burials in

76

purpose-dug graves and a few pits. Before considering the associations between these types of evidence, the chronology of the Iron Age activity needs to be clarified. Almost all of the pottery belongs to the early Iron Age, yet only one or two pits are securely dated to this phase.

The roundhouse

Few of the postholes contain any quantity of pottery, and the sherds are often small and thus potentially residual. There were however enough early Iron Age sizeable sherds from the porch, inner and outer ring postholes of the roundhouse to be fairly confident that this structure should be dated to the early Iron Age. One posthole from the alternative ring, presumably a different phase of the building, contained early-middle Iron Age pottery.

The main post-ring of the roundhouse (Grp 2719) is approximately 11 m in diameter, as is the possible alternative ring (Grp 2722). On the east side the structure was cut through by two Roman ditches, making it impossible to determine the total number and spacing of posts, but on the west, north and south the evidence is clearer. Most of the postholes of the main ring are roughly 2.5 m apart (centre to centre), though there also appear to be clusters only 1 m apart and gaps of up to 3 m in other places. It is however possible that one of the close-spaced groups on the east and west belong to the alternative ring, though this would still mean gaps of only 2 m in these areas. The alternative ring is more evenly spaced, the posts being mostly around 3 m apart, with one or two slightly wider gaps. The entrance posts are 2.7 m and 3.0 m apart, so that the entrance itself must have been between 2.2 m and 2.7 m wide.

There is an inner ring within the roundhouse approximately 8 m in diameter, most of the posts spaced at 1.5–2 m intervals, but with a 3 m gap on the north-west. This is slightly oval, being 1.5 m or less from the main post-ring at the north and south, but 2 m on the west.

The entrance to the roundhouse is on the south. This is a relatively uncommon orientation, the vast majority of roundhouses in the Upper Thames Valley having entrances that face either east or south-east (Hingley and Miles 1984, 63; Oswald 1997, fig. 10.2). Recently both Fitzpatrick (1997) and Oswald (1997) have suggested that this preference has symbolic significance, although Oswald has pointed out that on some sites interrelationships between buildings appear to be more important than other considerations. This appears to be the case with another local south-facing house at Hardwick, Oxon. (Allen and Robinson 1993), but no such factors are evident from the excavated area at Spring Road.

The postholes forming an outer ring may indicate an approximate diameter of 14 m. The spacing of the outer ring posts varies widely, as does the diameter of the postholes. It is difficult to construct a roundhouse of this diameter without an inner ring of posts, and more so if the outer ring does not have evenly

spaced substantial posts, so if genuine it is more likely that this outer ring was part of an aisled building rather than forming the only roof supports. If contemporary with the main ring of posts in any phase, however, the aisle between this and the main ring(s) of posts would have been little more than 1 m on the west, though perhaps as much as 2 m on the north and east sides. Since the main weight of an aisled structure is taken by the inner ring-beam, this is not structurally impossible, but means that the wall height would have varied around the building, and would imply that the outer wall was constructed after the inner ring.

A structure of this size would have required a substantial inner ring of posts to support the roof, and the postholes of the main ring are not uniformly large. It is possible that additional support for the roof was provided by some or all of the groups of postholes at the centre of the house, as was suggested for the house at Little Woodbury (Musson 1970). On that site, however, there was a square of large postholes, whereas the post-lines within the house at this site are mostly small, and better interpreted as internal partitions or furnishings. It is therefore alternatively possible that this outer ring was either for posts for a fence around the house, or for posts for partitions around the exterior, possibly for storage under the eaves.

The Iron Age burials

Three largely complete burials, one also including bones from an infant, were found within the area enclosed by the house, although the head of burial 2241 was missing, and in the relevant place was a posthole attributed to the latest phase of the structure, which might suggest that the burials were earlier. In fact, the burials all date to the 4th or 3rd century BC, and although different authorities have proposed different end dates for early Iron Age ceramics (Harding 1972; Lambrick 1984), only the very end of the early Iron Age overlaps with the date range of these burials, most of the range belonging with middle Iron Age ceramic forms and fabrics. These burials are therefore unlikely to have been foundation burials, and it is doubtful whether they were made while the structure was still in use. If the burials were directly connected with the building, as their position suggests, they may either have been made when the structure went out of use, possibly as propitiatory rituals, or have made use of the still-standing walls to help mark out what was a new type of burial in this part of Britain in the Iron Age, perhaps requiring its own particular rituals of separation and containment.

A possible parallel for this situation exists less than 5 km to the west at Noah's Ark, Frilford, where the crouched burial of a young adolescent and fragments of a new-born child were buried close to the north and south sides respectively of a stake-circle 9.5 m in diameter with an entrance 2 m wide on the south-east side (Harding 1987, fig. 3 and pages 7–8). Both early and middle Iron Age pottery was recovered from this site, but the predominance of middle Iron Age forms and fabrics led Harding to date the stake-circle and burials to the 2nd-1st centuries BC (ibid., 12–13). In his earlier thesis, Harding had interpreted the burials as being associated with the circle, and having a ritual purpose (Harding 1972, 64), but in his later report he revised this view, and due to its large size and the use of stakes generally less than 150 mm in diameter, interpreted the stake-circle not as a house but as a pen or enclosure of some sort (Harding 1987, 7–9). The significance of the associated burials is not further commented upon.

Another possible association of a posthole building and a burial occurred at Barton Court Farm on the east side of Abingdon. Here a crouched inhumation was found within an area of postholes possibly defining a circular building, though due to truncation by Roman features the shape was not entirely clear (Miles 1986, Microfiche C: 3–4 and fig. 76). The structure was dated to the late Iron Age, but the burial was undated, and though believed to be contemporary, may possibly have been earlier.

Although only three have been excavated, this group of purpose-dug graves can be described as a small cemetery of 3rd or 4th century BC date. In addition to the dated skeletons, there were at least two more crouched burials found, one some 60 m to the west accompanied by sherds of early Iron Age pottery, another a similar distance to the north-west in 1999. Given the presence of a Beaker crouched burial accompanied only by an awl, it is clearly impossible to be certain that the latter grave was not Bronze Age or even Neolithic, but further Iron Age burials on the site seem probable.

The three largely complete skeletons include two individuals crouched on their sides, and one laid on his back with the knees drawn up and the head bent forward, resting on the end of the grave. This could be viewed simply as a crouched burial in the vertical plane, but a range of skeletons in seated, bent over and other positions have been found recently in France, mirroring images on potin coins and statuettes, suggesting that such variations in the position of the dead are more significant (Lambot 2000). One of Lambot's interpretations for a group of sitting burials was that these were buried facing the rising sun. At Spring Road the individual buried on his back was facing due south, not towards the rising sun, but on the same orientation as the roundhouse within whose area the burials were found. The orientations of the bodies at Spring Road varied, the other young adult male having his head to the west-north-west, the child with its head to the south-east.

The child and the adult on his back were both moderately crouched, the knees of the other adult (skeleton 2243) were more tightly drawn up, probably to fit into the relatively narrow grave. None of the skeletons however showed signs of having been bound. It is unclear whether the head of skeleton 2243 was removed before burial, as the grave profile itself might suggest, or whether a shallower and

narrower slot had been excavated upon which to rest the head before it was cut through by a later posthole.

The infant bones included with the child burial are very unlikely to have been incorporated accidentally. No stray human bones were recovered from other features within the excavation area, so it is likely that the infant bones were purposely gathered and included in the grave. The presence of only part of the skeleton could partly be the result of later truncation, but this infant was not recognised as a group of articulated bones within the grave fill, suggesting that bones were gathered for incorporation after the body had become disarticulated. Both immediate burial of complete bodies and exposure followed later by partial burial therefore appear to have been contemporary rites in local Iron Age society.

Groups of skeletons in purpose-dug graves (in other words cemeteries) were until recently unknown in the Upper Thames Valley. A group of 35 inhumations in purpose-dug graves at Yarnton, Oxfordshire, has however recently been shown through radio-carbon dating to be 4th or 3rd century BC (Hey *et al.* 1999). Almost all of the graves were crouched or flexed, oriented north-south, and all were without grave-goods. The graves represent a mixture of adult men, women, adolescents and children, and are interpreted as a representative cross-section of the local population (see also 'Detailed report', Table 17). Only neonates were not included; these were buried separately within the adjacent settlement. Amongst the Yarnton burials there were two distinct concentrations 20 m apart, one of 15 graves in an area 14 m by 25 m, the other of 10 graves in an area 25 m by 25 m, with the remaining 10 inhumations scattered over a wider area. The concentrations were not in neat rows, though some immediately adjacent graves were aligned with one another.

The character of the Yarnton cemetery may provide a model for the type of cemetery found at this site, with small groups of clustered burials just outside the contemporary settlement focus and a wider scatter of others around the periphery of the settlement itself. At Spring Road the date of the burials may reflect the end of Iron Age occupation at the site, but this is not the case at Yarnton, where the settlement continued until the end of the Iron Age. The similar date range of the two cemeteries may instead represent the common adoption of a new burial rite in this part of the Upper Thames Valley during the middle Iron Age, though on the limited evidence available it does not appear to have lasted for long.

Early Iron Age settlements are now known to be numerous in and around Abingdon, indeed a pattern of sites no more than 2 km apart is now evident on the gravel terraces, situated alongside the north-south tributaries draining into the rivers Ock and Thames (Fig. 46). The settlement at Spring Road is imperfectly known, but on present evidence is different from neighbouring settlements such as Ashville/Wyndyke Furlong, where there were substantial numbers of enclosures surrounded by gullies and numerous deep circular pits. Only a single such pit was found within the Spring Road excavated area, although a scatter of others were reported by the cemetery gravediggers, and have produced pottery to support this dating (see for instance Fig. 31, 13). The fragmentary curving gully at the north end of Area 8 may indicate another roundhouse enclosure, but the absence of any Iron Age activity in Area 5 makes it unlikely that the excavated site lay at the edge of a dense cluster of pits and roundhouse gullies like those at Ashville or Wyndyke Furlong across the Larkhill Stream, or at Gravelly Guy, Stanton Harcourt (Parrington 1978; Muir and Roberts 1999; Lambrick and Allen 2005).

Very little evidence of the environment and economy of the Iron Age settlement was recovered. The animal bones indicated the presence of the main domesticates, with sheep predominating, as occurred at Ashville and Wyndyke Furlong nearby (Wilson in Parrington 1978, 136). One tree-throw hole contained a large sherd of late Bronze Age/early Iron Age pottery, and if not residual, this may indicate that some trees had established themselves on the site, possibly following a phase of ploughing in the late Bronze Age, and were then cleared to make way for the settlement. Charcoal indicates the presence of oak woodland, together with hawthorn, in the vicinity (Chapter 4).

Other than the burials, there is one pit tentatively dated to the middle Iron Age on the basis of the pottery fabrics (605). This sparse evidence possibly indicates that settlement was becoming nucleated at the extensive Ashville/Wyndyke Furlong site. A similar process of nucleation has been suggested under Abingdon town centre with the apparent abandonment of the early Iron Age site at Audlett Drive (Keevill 1992), and the expansion of the Vineyard settlement adjacent (Allen 2000, 11).

Following the discovery of a late Iron Age/early Roman defended oppidum under the town centre, the pottery from Ashville (De Roche 1978) has been reassessed, and it is now clear that occupation continued on that site through the late Iron Age and into the early Roman period (Timby 1999, 38). It would therefore appear that settlement continued to be concentrated west of the Larkhill Stream until the late 1st/early 2nd century AD, when occupation again becomes evident at Spring Road.

THE ROMAN ENCLOSURE SYSTEM IN AREAS 8 AND 9
by Zena Kamash and Tim Allen

Extent of the Roman occupation

A series of coaxial/rectilinear ditches, gullies and fence-lines define the 2nd- and 3rd-century occupation at Spring Road. The ditches of this system continued northwards, southwards and westwards beyond the limits of excavation, and were truncated on the east by medieval pits. There are no cropmarks

visible within the cemetery site to throw light on the wider form of the settlement, and to the south the ground was taken over by burials, but geophysical survey did reveal linear anomalies on the same alignment within the allotments to the west that could well represent further enclosures (Fig. 42). Beyond the cemetery site north of this there is a significant drop in ground level, apparently created when the adjacent school was built, which may have truncated any archaeological features, as there were no geophysical anomalies in this area. The absence of similar gullies or any Roman activity in the northernmost excavation area (Area 5) may however indicate that this was close to the northern limit of the settlement; there was also a dearth of archaeological activity in the evaluation trench dug in 1990 west of Area 5.

Date and status of the Roman activity

The phasing is complicated by the presence of two later-4th-century coins found in the ditches. The AE3 Valens coin from context 1154 (intervention 1153) came from the secondary fill of the ditch, which might have been open for a considerable length of time, or might have incorporated later material falling down cracks or carried down by root action. The coin from 1098 (intervention 1099) is more problematic as it came from low down within the ditch, and from a fill otherwise containing a large deposit of unabraded 2nd- and 3rd-century pottery. The surface condition of the coin (a brassy finish, and cleaned surface with no corrosion), seems extraordinary considering the soil from which it was apparently recovered, and suggests that it was planted in the ditch and actually has an unknown provenance.

The Roman pottery is typical of low-status sites; there are few fine and specialist wares, items like the *mortaria* being found on almost every low-status site in the region (Henig and Booth 2000, 153). The lack of more prestigious wares and other luxury metal items suggests that the site was rural and low-status in character.

Layout and orientation of the enclosures

The ditches and gullies are oriented predominantly on a NNW – SSE and ENE – WSW alignment, the system dating to the 2nd century AD. In the western half of the excavated area this alignment was superseded by two ditches forming a new boundary on a NNE – SSW and ESE – WNW alignment in the late-2nd century/early-3rd century. It is clear that the later system was tacked onto the earlier, as the ditches of the later alignment join those of the earlier at the north end of the excavation, and a ditch at right angles to this later boundary stops short of the earlier boundary, creating a triangular enclosure between them. A parallel for this oddly-shaped enclosure may have existed locally at Appleford Field (Hinchcliffe and Thomas 1980, figs 3 and 13), where

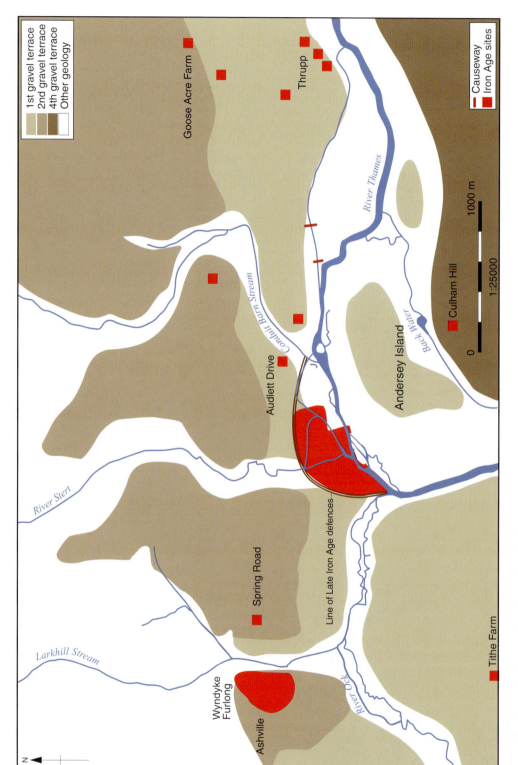

Figure 46   Spring Road in relation to Iron Age sites in the area.

the trackway and enclosure boundaries converged north of the excavated area. Although at Spring Road the later boundaries do not physically cut ditches of the earlier system, they cut diagonally across enclosures of the earlier system, and had the earlier enclosure boundaries still been extant, would have created small and irregular-shaped areas between them. It is therefore likely that the earlier enclosures west of the main NNW-SSE boundary went out of use at this time.

The alignment of the enclosures may have been based upon the course of the Larkhill Stream, which runs southwards towards the river Ock only 200 m or so to the west (see Fig. 47). Nowadays this stream runs SSE from the A34 north of the site, veering to the SSW as it passes the site, and then kinking SSE again south of Spring Road down to the Ock. If the stream has not changed its course, it is possible that the earlier alignment of Roman ditches was related to the line of the Larkhill Stream as it approached the site from the north; locals report much Roman material observed when the playing field was constructed, and the settlement may have continued, and the boundaries have been laid out, from a focus further to the north-west. The later shift in alignment may have been to realign the settlement with the line of the Larkhill Stream immediately west of the site, as the stream changes course below the junction of its two arms, which lay approximately opposite the junction of the two boundary ditches at Spring Road.

West of the Larkhill Stream the Roman boundaries revealed by excavations at Ashville (Parrington 1978) and Wyndyke Furlong (Muir and Roberts 1999) are rather fragmentary, but appear to follow a predominantly north-south alignment (Fig. 47). Those closest to the line of the stream do not respect its line, but are aligned either side of a trackway, which if projected would suggest a crossing point to the north beneath the modern A34. This alignment began with a small middle Iron Age enclosure (Muir and Roberts 1999, Figure 2.4), and was reinforced by the appearance of trackway ditches and adjacent enclosures or fields in the 1st century AD, so the crossing and alignment was in existence before the Roman settlement on the Spring Road side began.

Further south at Wyndyke Furlong an early Roman boundary ditch ran east-west approximately in line with the junction of the two arms of the Larkhill Stream. The early Roman ditches at Ashville ran slightly south of east, again at right angles to the adjacent stream, but the 2nd century Roman ditches run more NNW, parallel to those at Spring Road across the river. A limited watching brief upon construction at Lambourn Court also revealed ditches on an approximately N-S alignment, which although undated were probably also parts of this system.

At Spring Road this network of ditches, gullies and fence-lines created at least five 2nd-century enclosures and three late-2nd/early-3rd-century enclosures (Figs 15–16). The 2nd-century enclosures were rectangular or almost square and varied in size from 20.2 m by 11.2 m to 23.2 m by 25.2 m. No whole late-2nd-/early-3rd-century enclosures were revealed in their entirety, but they also seem to have been rectangular or square. From the elements of these later enclosures that are visible, it seems likely that they were of similar dimensions to the earlier enclosures. A group of three possible rectangular enclosures were indicated by the geophysical survey to the west, all approximately 36 m east-west by 19 or 20 m north-south.

A small group of subrectangular enclosures were found in the late Iron Age and Roman phases at Ashville over the Larkhill Stream to the west (Parrington 1978, figs 2 and 3). These were slightly larger, from 32 by 27 m up to c 37 by 40 m (minimum), and were defined by much more substantial ditches. At the Vineyard in central Abingdon the settlement within the late Iron Age and early Roman defensive ditches was laid out as a series of rectangular or subrectangular enclosures. The layout was modified frequently, and few complete enclosures survived the later digging of a medieval moat, but several enclosures were 11–12 m wide and 23–25 m long (Allen 1990, fig. 3). The Spring Road enclosures are also comparable to the small later 2nd-century enclosures excavated at Roughground Farm, Lechlade, Gloucestershire, which measured 17 m by 27 m (Allen *et al.* 1993, 187).

The fence-lines are generally either parallel to or at right angles to the ditches and gullies, and sometimes continue their lines, acting as extensions. Despite the shortage of Roman finds from the postholes, one of these alignments (631) is stratigraphically earlier than a Roman ditch, and it is therefore likely that many of the others are also Roman. The use of fences as extensions for ditched enclosures has also been noted locally at Gravelly Guy, Stanton Harcourt in association with 1st-century AD enclosures (Lambrick and Allen 2005).

Nature and function of the site

The enclosures at Ashville were interpreted by the excavator as a series of fields (Parrington 1978, 36), although he recognised that some of them were associated with pits, and a large assemblage of pottery was recovered in fresh condition from both ditches and pits. This last association suggests that a settlement focus lay very close by, and these enclosures may have been part of the settlement complex itself. Ditches at the north end of Wyndyke Furlong and at Lambourn Court, however, which had few associated features and contained few finds, are more likely to be field boundaries. Clear examples of Roman fields with preserved ploughsoils or ard marks have been identified at Drayton Cursus and at Yarnton (Barclay *et al.* 2003; Hey 1993, 84). In neither case were there associated features, and finds from the ditches were few. The Roman fields at Drayton, which were used first for arable and later for pasture, were 90 m wide and at least as long; those at Yarnton generally more than 100 m in either direction (Hey pers. comm.). Although 'Celtic'

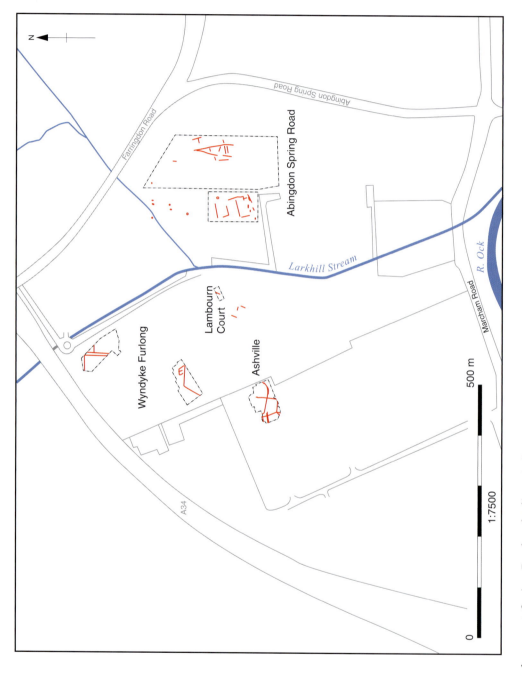

Figure 47 Roman enclosures at Spring Road and adjacent sites.

fields are small, the Spring Road enclosures are clearly too small to have functioned effectively as fields. At Yarnton a line of small rectangular enclosures around 25 m by 40 m were found, but these lay adjacent to the main domestic enclosures, and were clearly part of the settlement.

With the exception of the fence-lines, no coherent structures could be discerned from the palimpsest of postholes at Spring Road. One reason for the lack of identifiable structures, which are also lacking in many other 1st and 2nd century rural low-status settlements in Oxfordshire, may be the techniques used in the construction of buildings of this period. At the Vineyard in central Abingdon, where huge quantities of domestic debris were recovered from the ditches, no post-built buildings were identified, although painted wall daub with wattle impressions indicates that buildings were present. A subrectangular platform of cobbles of Iron Age origin, remade twice into the early Roman period, may however indicate timber-sill construction. Buildings constructed upon horizontal timber sills, whose shallow timber slots survived, were found at Dorchester-on-Thames nearby (Frere 1984), but evidence of this type is unlikely to have survived the ploughing at Spring Road.

At Gravelly Guy, Stanton Harcourt, Oxfordshire, four 1st-century AD enclosures were excavated, none of which contained structural evidence (Lambrick and Allen 2005). It was however suggested that these enclosures did contain structures that may have been mass-walled, as at Hod Hill in Dorset (Richmond 1968). Mass-wall construction techniques, such as cob construction, build from ground-level or require only shallowly-based posts, and therefore leave little or no trace below ground (Henig and Booth 2000, 82).

Despite the lack of structural evidence it is likely that the small enclosures at Spring Road related to domestic activity, due to the concentrations of pottery, including partly reconstructible vessels, at the terminals of two ditches at right angles, ditch group 1627 (cut 1077) and group 1629 (intervention 1101). The two almost certainly form part of one enclosure. The only other sizeable pottery assemblage came from a secondary fill within ditch group 1626 (cut 1153), and may also have been contemporary debris. This is corroborated by the animal bone evidence, which suggests that human activity was concentrated around these main ditches and around posthole groups 2715 and 2716 (Chapter 4).

Concentrations of domestic finds at the terminals of penannular gullies of the Iron Age have long been argued to indicate house sites (eg at Roughground Farm, Lechlade, Gloucestershire, Allen *et al.* 1993, 51 and 179; see also Allen *et al.* 1984, fig. 6.3). This pattern also appears to continue into the early Roman period: at Old Shifford Farm, for instance, domestic debris was concentrated at the terminals of a succession of D-shaped enclosures containing postholes, argued to represent a house-site (Hey 1995, 102–12 and 168–9). Similar patterns of deposition were also

noted at the Vicarage Field, Stanton Harcourt, Oxfordshire (Thomas 1955, 9–11).

The other ditches and gullies on the site, however, contained little or no pottery. This is unlikely to be the result of later recutting, of which there is little evidence on the site, and since the large assemblages of finds from ditches came from throughout their fills, only the shallowest gullies may possibly have had the character of their fills significantly affected by later truncation. For the 2nd century phase it is therefore possible either that the focus of the 2nd-century domestic activity lay outside the excavation area, perhaps destroyed by the medieval gravel-extraction pits to the east, or that the enclosures were fields and there was no domestic activity on the site at this time. The gravel-pits do not, however, seem to account satisfactorily for the low density of postholes in the eastern sector of the site because north of the pits in Area 8 there is also a lack of postholes. It would seem then that the postholes are restricted by the central Roman ditches to the western sector of the site.

Market garden plots, storage areas or paddocks for containing animals with young are possible other uses given the small size of these enclosures. Although some of the ditches seem too shallow to have acted as barriers for animals, particularly those in the north-east of Area 8 (groups 2583, 2584, 2585 and 2586), parallel fence-lines may in some cases have provided further barriers, and others may have been accompanied by hedges. Evidence for hedges usually takes the form of shallow irregular linear disturbances, which may not have survived later truncation. Charcoal from the site did however indicate three species of thorny shrub that could have come from hedges (Chapter 4).

Environmental evidence for the settlement overall is limited. Charcoal indicates that both oak and beech were present in the vicinity – the latter the first positive identification in the Upper Thames Valley during this period – and several species of thorny shrub (Chapter 4). Animal bones show the presence of the main domesticates, with sheep continuing to predominate (Chapter 4). This is a pattern also shared by the Roman settlement at Abingdon Vineyard below the town centre, but not by Barton Court Farm to the east of the town, where cattle become more important in the Roman period (Wilson in Miles 1986). Charred plant remains were few, but include spelt wheat in one of the ditches; this is the preferred variety in the Iron Age, but was increasingly supplanted by bread wheat during the Roman period, for instance at Barton Court Farm. Overall the impression is of a traditional pattern of farming continuing late prehistoric practices.

The Roman enclosure system in its wider context (Fig. 48)

The Spring Road site has a very different Roman history compared to most other sites in the Abingdon area. Abingdon, like Dorchester-on-Thames, was very important at the end of the Iron Age and saw

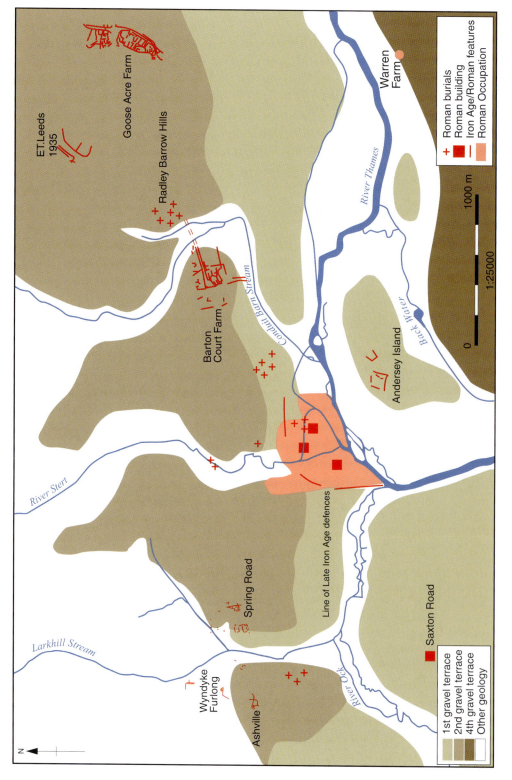

Figure 48 Roman sites around Abingdon.

continued occupation into the early Roman period (Henig and Booth 2000, 75). Many of the early Roman sites previously excavated in the Abingdon area however show evidence of an hiatus or at least a significant decrease in activity in the mid-2nd century AD: Ashville Trading Estate/Wyndyke Furlong (Parrington 1978, 36; reinterpretation of the ceramic evidence: Henig and Booth 2000, 107; Muir and Roberts 1999, 37), Barton Court Farm (Miles 1986, 49; Henig and Booth 2000, 84), Eight Acre Field, Radley (Mudd *et al.* 1995, 38), Drayton North Cursus (Barclay *et al.* 2003) and even Abingdon town centre (Henig and Booth 2000, 71 discussing Abingdon Vineyard). It has been suggested that this may have been due to Frilford/Marcham supplanting Abingdon as a local centre because Frilford/Marcham was much closer to a major Roman road (Henig and Booth 2000, 75).

At Spring Road, however, the ceramic evidence points to a clear hiatus in settlement from the end of the middle Iron Age until the 2nd century AD, and occupation limited to the 2nd and 3rd centuries AD. A break in occupation on long-established sites at around AD 130 is also evident across much of the Upper Thames Valley (Henig and Booth 2000, 106), and as a corollary a substantial number of rural settlement sites were established in the 2nd century AD and remained stable into the later Roman period (*ibid.*). It would seem, therefore, that Spring Road falls into this latter group of sites, possibly acting as a new focus for the group formerly settled at Ashville.

The reason for this mid-2nd-century dislocation in Abingdon is not entirely clear. Although it is still possible that Abingdon saw a decrease in importance in the mid-2nd century with the rise of Frilford/Marcham as a new local centre, why should activity diminish on established sites and new activity occur on alternative sites? As Henig and Booth point out, none of the listed early Roman settlements that apparently show a hiatus has been completely excavated, and the dating of the apparent re-planning is not precise. It is alternatively possible that these settlements shifted focus individually over a few decades. Locally it may be more of a change in character of existing settlements, or at least only very local movement within farming units, than complete abandonment and relocation.

Within Abingdon town new masonry Romanised buildings were being erected at Abingdon Vineyard and East St. Helen's Street early in the second century (Allen 1990, 74; Wilson and Wallis 1991), and at the periphery of the town there was clearly an expansion in the area of Roman settlement in the second century, concomitant with the apparent decline in intensity of activity in areas occupied in the 1st century AD. It may be that the appearance of these Romanised buildings marks the movement of the local aristocracy into the town, and a reorganisation of rural estates including the creation of separate, new settlements for the farm workers. The Spring Road settlement may therefore be an expression of this new social order, part of what Lambrick described as 'a further stage in a process of break up of earlier, Iron Age structures, in the context of a more capital intensive system involving a much more complex social, economic and political infrastructure' (Lambrick 1992, 105; Henig and Booth 2000, 109–110). Other rural settlements around Abingdon that on present evidence may appear in the 2nd century include one at Radley (Benson and Miles 1974, map 31), an enclosure on Andersey Island (Ainslie 1991), and possibly the line of enclosures or 'ladder-settlement' east of Gooseacre Farm, Radley (Benson and Miles 1974, map 31).

SAXON PERIOD
by Zena Kamash and Tim Allen

The Saxon period at Spring Road was represented by two sunken-featured buildings in Area 8 and other concentrations of Saxon pottery in Areas 3 and 4. In addition, one pit of Saxon date was identified in Area 9 during the 1994 AAAHS excavations. All of these features and their associated finds appear to be of 6th-century date. Fifth-century domestic activity is known from the centre of town at the Vineyard, and early 5th-century burials were found at the Saxton Road cemetery only some 600 m from the site south of the river Ock (Leeds and Harden 1936, 5; Chadwick Hawkes 1986, 73–4), but on present evidence the Saxon activity at Spring Road appears to represent a 6th century re-occupation of a site not inhabited since Roman times, unlike the suggested continuity at Barton Court Farm east of Abingdon (Miles 1986, 51).

The sunken-featured buildings (SFBs)

Both SFBs (2008 in the north and 2687 in the south) were rectangular with rounded corners and had dimensions of 3.05 m by 2.26 m by 0.28 m (2008) and 3.12 m by 2.90 m by 0.26 m. These dimensions are approximately average for SFBs and are comparable to two out of three SFBs found beyond St Helen's Church to the south in Abingdon (Rahtz 1976, 75 and app. 1, 408). Three slightly smaller and square SFBs have been excavated at Audlett Drive, Abingdon (Keevill 1992, 62). In addition, seven larger SFBs (*c* 3 m by 4 m) were excavated at Barton Court Farm, Abingdon (Miles 1986, 16). Other SFBs identified in the surrounding area include 2 from the Abingdon Vineyard excavations, 60 from Barrow Hills, Radley and 33 from Sutton Courtenay (Allen 1990, 74; Chambers and Halpin 1986, 111; Leeds 1947, 79) (see Fig. 49). The southern SFB (2687) at Spring Road typically had the postholes in its short sides on the east-west axis. This is the commonest type of SFB (Rahtz 1976, 75); at Mucking and West Stow, for example, the highest proportion of SFBs were of this type (Hamerow 1993, 10; West 1985, 113). The two postholes have been interpreted as ridge-pole supports (Rahtz 1976, 75).

The northern SFB (2008) was slightly atypical since there were two postholes in the western end. This is a rare phenomenon, but can be paralleled at Mucking, Essex where seven SFBs out of a total of 203 had double gable posts (Hamerow 1993, 10f). Both of the Spring Road SFBs appeared to contain additional posts, and in 2687 there were also possible postpads. Only eight SFBs at Mucking had additional supporting posts set within the floor area (Hamerow 1993, 11), but this feature was also present at locally at Barton Court Farm and at Audlett Drive (Miles 1986, 35; Keevill 1992, 62). As Keevill notes, if these posts are additional supports for the ridge pole, then they preclude the provision of a suspended floor above the pit (1992, 77). There are however no clues at Spring Road as to what function these additional posts may have served, nor is it certain that they were contemporary with the use of the structures.

The function of the SFBs at Spring Road is also uncertain. Weaving equipment is often associated with SFBs (Rahtz 1976, 76); local examples occur at both the Abingdon Vineyard and at Barton Court Farm (Allen 1990, 74; Miles 1986, 35). At Spring Road, however, neither SFB produced artefacts associated with weaving. The animal bone assemblages from the SFBs do show more evidence of butchery than other bone assemblages on the site (Chapter 4: Charles). The assemblages are still mixed, however, and are more likely to represent mixed domestic debris than solely butchery debris (*ibid.*). Overall, both the small and large animal bone assemblages probably derived from general domestic activity, rather than special or specific activities. Furthermore, as noted at Barton Court Farm, 'it is dangerous to draw conclusions about the function of buildings on the basis of re-deposited rubbish within them' (Miles 1986, 35).

There is a marked difference between the deposition patterns of the SFBs. Although very similar in depth to 2687, and unlikely to have been truncated to a greater degree, SFB 2008 contained only one fill, whereas 2687 contained three fills. In addition, SFB 2687 produced more than 4.5 times the amount of pottery than 2008 (Table 9). A similar discrepancy is visible in the large animal bone assemblage, three times as many animal bones coming from 2687 than from 2008.

The upper fills of SFB 2687 contained the majority of the ecofactual and artefactual material. A cross-fitting sherd between layer 2672 within 2687 and

modern grave 3511 (4 M 7) indicates either that a Saxon feature contemporary with the backfilling of the SFB was disturbed by the modern grave, or that some rubbish was dug out and redeposited on occasions. Given the relatively well-preserved sherds from these upper fills, the former seems more likely in this case.

The animal bone and pottery assemblages from the primary fill (2686) of 2687 were much smaller, and the average sherd size was also smaller. The primary fill of 2687 was 0.3 m thick, thicker than the two upper fills, and this emphasises the low density of material within this deposit. This fill was also more compacted than the layers above, perhaps indicating a build up of soil over a considerable length of time. The character of this deposit suggests that the SFB was left open for some time before being back-filled with rubbish, and so might have been in use somewhat earlier than the material dumped in its upper fills.

The greater compaction of this deposit, and the smaller size of the finds within it, could alternatively be interpreted as indicating an *in situ* accumulation of occupation debris on or below the floor. The lack of surfaces within the deposit, however, or of clear horizons of occupation material, argues against the former. At Barton Court Farm there was no trace of build-up of occupation debris and the excavator felt that this was due to the fact that the 'huts' must have been cleaned regularly (Miles 1986, 35). At Mucking, the majority of finds and workshop debris came from upper fills, and it was thought that only very few SFBs contained an occupation layer (Hamerow 1993, 14). At West Stow, however, more finds were recorded from the primary fills, which were fine-grained and homogeneous, leading the excavator to believe that the primary fill did not represent the use of the pit as a refuse dump after it had gone out of use, but consisted of material that had accumulated below the suspended plank floor of the building during use (West 1985, 119). This pattern of infill could however indicate that SFBs were reused for rubbish-disposal immediately, rather than that the finds necessarily derive from *in situ* activity. With only two SFBs at Spring Road it is impossible to deduce a pattern to the use of these structures at this site.

Table 9 Comparison of finds from Sunken-Featured Buildings 2687 and 2008.

Material	SFB 2687					SFB 2008	
	2686 primary	2673 secondary	2703 finds ref.	2672 tertiary	SFB 2687 Total	2009=2010=2479=2480	SFB 2008 Total
Pottery	15 (185 g)	81 (1503 g)	50 (798 g)	147 (2287 g)	293 (4727 g)	55 (1025 g)	55 (1025 g)
Animal bone (bulk)	23	158	177	604	357	114	114
Animal bone (sieved)	125	522	–	201	848	394	394

The features potentially associated with the SFBs at Spring Road are also of interest. Both SFBs have postholes around the outside of the pit (see Fig. 14), although as these are not clearly dated they may not be contemporary. Despite looking for evidence for external walls, none was found at Barrow Hills, Radley nor at Barton Court Farm (Chambers and Halpin 1986, 111; Miles 1986, 35). If genuinely associated, these might lend support to West's interpretation of SFBs as larger timber buildings with partly-cellared interiors, although West himself argues that postholes for earth-fast posts are mainly of value during construction, and are not really necessary once the building is up (West 2001, 72). These postholes could however simply represent fenced areas surrounding the structures.

Several of the tentative lines of postholes within the site contained small Saxon sherds, and it is possible that these were Saxon fence lines. The fact that these fence lines share the same alignment as Roman ditches may be due to the persistence of these boundaries into the Late Roman and early Saxon period as hedges. At Barton Court Farm, Abingdon and Barrow Hills, Radley, fences rather than ditches formed enclosures around some of the

Saxon buildings (Miles 1986, 16–18 and fig. 13; Chambers and McAdam 2007, 68–9 and fig. 3.8). At both of these sites the sunken-featured buildings were accompanied by a variety of posthole rectangular buildings, although at Barton Court Farm even the best-preserved buildings were incomplete, and corner posts were frequently lacking. Similar structures might be expected at Spring Road, and it is possible to suggest tentative building outlines amongst the many postholes (Figs 14 and 15–16), although none is entirely convincing. Due to the uncertainty, however, further discussion is unwarranted.

A small quantity of fired clay, one fragment bearing a wattle impression, was found within one of the SFBs, but this need not have derived from the superstructure of the building. Generally fired clay and daub is only found at a few early to middle Anglo-Saxon sites (Hamerow 1993, 13), perhaps indicating that this was not the predominant material used for the walls of these structures. West did however find evidence of clay walling adjacent to hearths at West Stow (West 2001, 17, 22 and 72), and one internal oven, from which such fired clay could have derived.

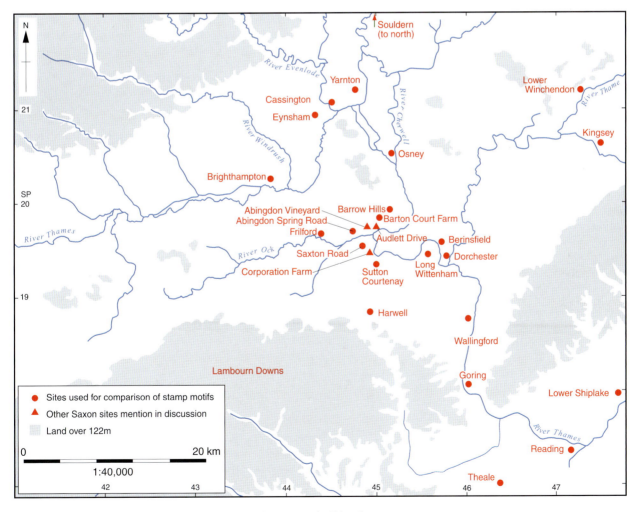

Figure 49   Spring Road in relation to Saxon sites around Abingdon.

The position of SFB 2687 astride the double Roman boundary ditches strongly suggests that this boundary had disappeared long before. The location of SFB 2008 within the middle Bronze Age timber circle is likely to be fortuitous. It has often been observed that older monuments were important to the Anglo-Saxons and it has been said that 'the correlation between important prehistoric sites of the [Upper Thames] region and the important Anglo-Saxon ones is uncanny.' (Blair 1994, xxiv, xxv). This can be seen for example at Barrow Hills, Radley, Sutton Courtenay and Saxton Road (Blair 1994, 20; Leeds 1947; Leeds and Harden 1936, 9). In this case, however, there is no evidence that the circle, or indeed a mound surrounded by it, would still have been in existence in the Anglo-Saxon period, and since there is no indication that SFB 2687 was dug into a mound, the similar depth of both SFBs at this site strongly suggests that there was none below 2008 either.

Of particular note, is a stamped unstratified sherd collected during modern grave-digging on the site. This sherd has been identified as having a 'like stamp' with another small sherd found at Sutton Courtenay some 9 km to the south (see Chapter 3, Fig. 38, and Fig. 49). A find of this kind is exceptionally rare. The sherd from Sutton Courtenay was retrieved during the latter phases of Leeds' excavations, but sadly no stratified location is given in the report (Leeds 1947, pl. XXII(b)). There is, however, a description of House XXI, which was much larger than the other SFBs excavated and which contained a 'basket-like pen with a large mass of clay' (Leeds 1947, 83). The presence of this installation led Leeds to interpret the 'house' as a potter's workshop on analogy with similar installations found at Dorchester (*ibid.*). It is tempting, but highly speculative, to suppose that the stamp was made in that workshop. What we can say with confidence is that some form of trade link existed between Sutton Courtenay and Spring Road, Abingdon, whether involving the pots themselves or the contents of the pots. The limited evidence from Spring Road, however, makes it very difficult to define further links between the two sites.

Considerable environmental evidence has been retrieved for the economy and environment of the Saxon settlement, even though it has come from only two buildings within the settlement. This indicates a mixed farming economy, with sheep and pigs predominant amongst the livestock, which may indicate more woodland locally than in previous periods. Sloe and hawthorn were amongst the charcoal, and were probably collected locally as fuel, as well as oak and hazel; both fruits and nuts may also have been harvested. The weeds of wet ground need only indicate the use of the lower-lying ground alongside the Larkhill Stream for fodder, though bread wheat, barley and either beans or peas were grown, and cultivated plots may have included these low-lying areas immediately adjacent to the site. A single eel bone suggests that the inhabitants also fished seasonally on the river Ock (Chapter 4).

MEDIEVAL AND POST-MEDIEVAL PERIODS
by Tim Allen

Groups of pits, some open at the same time, others intercutting, covered a considerable area down the east side of the site. Despite this, the excavated sample of these pits produced relatively few finds. The finds were very mixed and included pottery ranging in date from the Bronze Age to the 13th century AD, as well as animal bone and flint. The fills of the pits were either friable or loose sandy silt deposits or redeposited lenses of natural gravel, and the fills often spread between two or more intercutting pits. The low density of finds in the pits makes it highly unlikely that these pits were used for the deposition of rubbish. The irregular shapes and sizes of the pits also contrasts with the regular shape of cesspits and rubbish pits found associated with tenements in Abingdon.

One plausible interpretation was that these pits were dug in repeated visits to extract gravel on a small scale, possibly by individual householders. The lenses of redeposited natural gravel may seem rather anomalous, but several explanations present themselves: erosion of the sides of the pits over time, shovelling of gravel being extracted into adjacent partially-filled pits before carting it away or dumping of unwanted gravel back into open pits. Similarly irregular groups of pits have been observed during redevelopment of the MG works west of the Larkhill Stream, where they were dated to the late Roman period (Halpin pers. comm.), and on the east side of Abingdon Abbey precinct south of the Vineyard (OA 2005), where they also date to the 13th century.

The extent of these intercutting pits, and the wide date range of the pottery found within them, strongly suggests that they truncated or obliterated earlier features in this area of the site. This partly explains the low numbers of earlier prehistoric features on the site and the lack of Roman enclosure ditches in the south-eastern area of the site. While, however, the pits certainly contain residual material, this does not appear to occur in any obvious concentrations of one period or another. Furthermore, the pits do not seem to account satisfactorily for the low density of postholes in the eastern sector of the site, as the area north of the pits in Area 8 also contains few postholes. It would seem then that the postholes were restricted by the central Roman ditches to the western side of the site, perhaps indicating that the domestic activity was also concentrated west of the boundary.

The site lay outside the known limits of the town during the medieval period. In Munby's reconstruction of the medieval field system of Abingdon (Lambrick and Slade 1991, fig. 4) he does not name this particular land parcel, and it lies outside the main West or North fields of the town, though it lies adjacent to Hitching Field (Fig. 50). It is possible that this patch of ground was peripheral to the main three field system, either one of those fields reserved for additional cultivation depending upon local

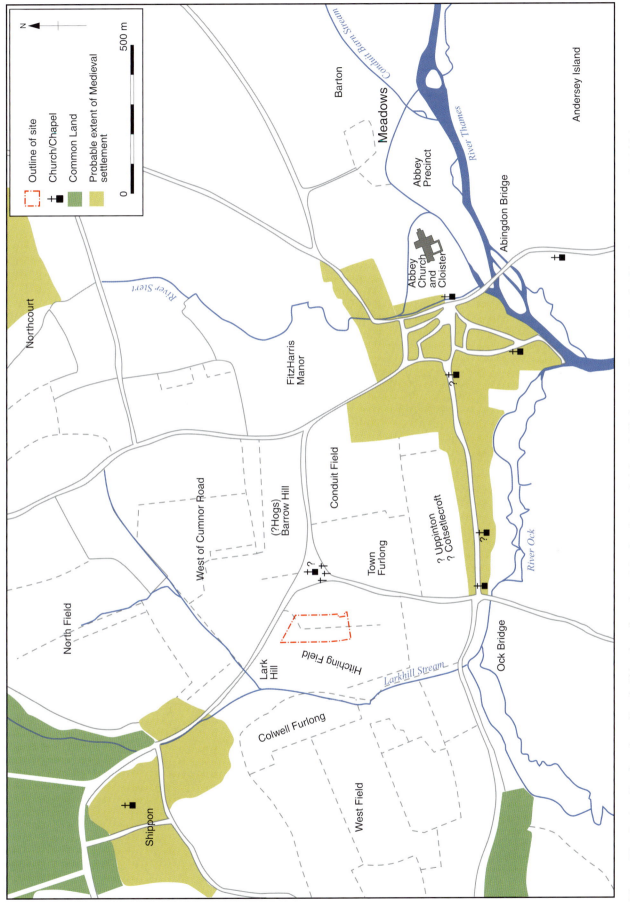

Figure 50   Spring Road and medieval Abingdon (based on Munby, in Lambrick and Slade 1991, fig.4 Medieval Abingdon: Town and Fields).

need, or reserved for grazing. Such an area might well be regarded as open to exploitation for other needs, such as gravel for local building projects. On present evidence, this exploitation did not last for long, as almost all of the medieval pottery dates to the 13th century. Wilson (Harman and Wilson 1981, 60–61) argued that deep pits found at the junction of Spring Road and Faringdon Road were gravel pits periodically used to repair borough roads, but the evidence from the Spring Road cemetery is consistent with a relatively short-lived but quite large-scale requirement for gravel, such as would have been needed for the construction of a chapel and burial ground at the road junction nearby (see Chapter 1).

The use of the site in the late medieval and early post-medieval period is unclear. The single extended burial found on the west edge of the site accompanied by a wound-wire headed pin most likely dates to the 16th or 17th centuries, though such pins

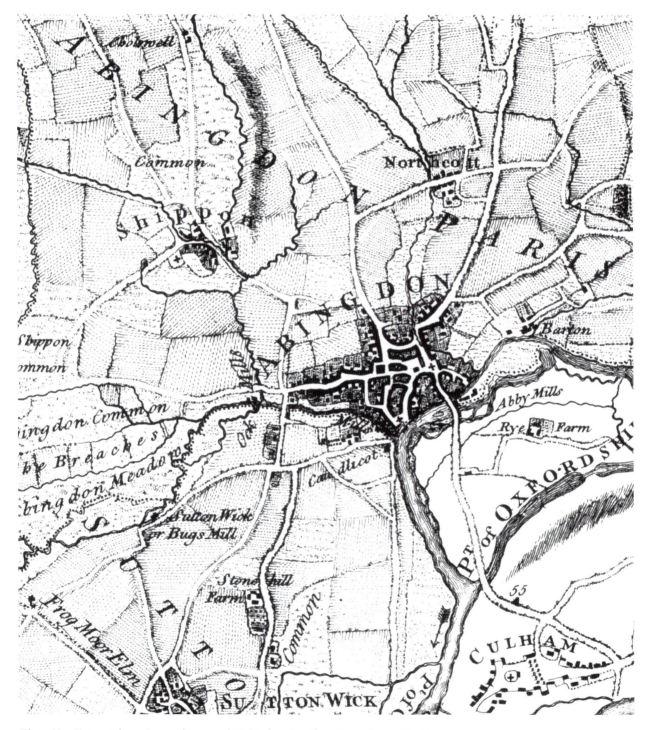

Plate 10 Extract from Rocque's map of 1761 showing the site under cultivation.

continued to be used for fastening as an alternative to buttons into the 18th or even the early 19th century. Wilson (*ibid*, 61) suggested that the burial ground at the road junction to the east went out of use towards the end of the 13th century, following the establishment of the Abbot of Abingdon's right to all mortuaries in the parish in 1284, but even if it continued in use into the post-medieval period, this burial lies over 200 m from the other known burials. It is possible that this was someone who could not be buried in consecrated ground, such as a suicide or criminal hanged on the gallows, or the victim of an unlawful killing, but a more plausible explanation, given the likely date, is that this was a casualty of the Civil War, buried after one of the many skirmishes around Abingdon, or a victim of the plague. Another lone burial probably of post-medieval date was found on the north side of Ock Street just east of Ock Bridge during redevelopment (SMR). The fact that a burial was made at Spring Road at a time when no field boundaries along this line existed (or at least were not indicated either by Rocque's map of 1761 or the early O.S. maps) perhaps indicates that this land

was not under cultivation at the time, although for a hurried burial this may not have mattered.

The origins of the 'headland' that was believed from the evaluation to run north-south down the site need further consideration. A depth of nearly 1 m of soil was found down the centre of the site, while less than half that depth of soil was found in evaluation Trench F, and indeed in excavation Area 5. From the excavations it is now clear that this soil overlies the 13th century gravel pits, and is cut by the late Victorian quarry. The quarry was not shown on the 1st edition Ordnance Survey map of 1873, nor on the 3rd edition of 1914, but does appear on the 2nd edition maps of 1900 and 1904 (Plate 11). It was clearly short lived, and probably opened purely to meet the short-term needs of local development, possibly at St. Helen's School, built between 1900 and 1914 just to the north.

Although it seemed plausible that the depth of soil had resulted from the creation of a medieval head-land, no trace of medieval furrows was found in either the excavations or evaluations. Moreover, the finds from all of the soils making up the 1 m

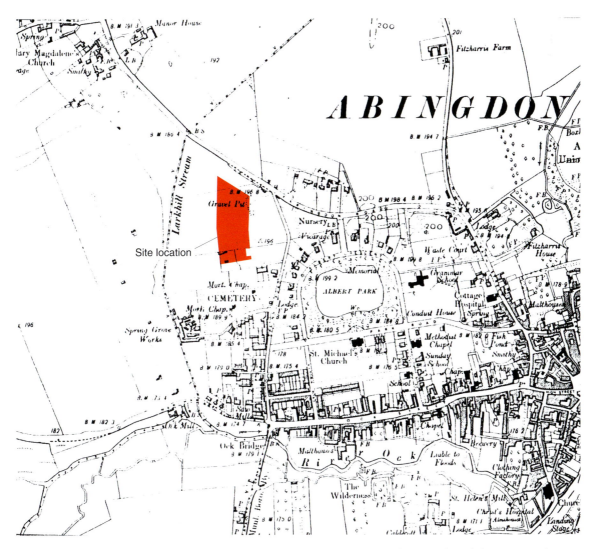

Plate 11   Extract from 2nd Edition OS map of 1904 showing gravel pit on the east edge of the current site.

accumulation contained post-medieval items, showing that the accumulation did not begin in earnest until at least the 17th century. Rocque's map of 1761 shows the site under cultivation (Plate 10), but there is no indication of a headland or other boundary, suggesting that the accumulation may have occurred later still. No boundary is shown on the Christ's Hospital map of 1835, though as this map does not show detail in this area this may not be relevant. There is similarly no boundary indicated on the 1st edition Ordnance Survey may of 1873. It remains possible that a boundary was established in the late 18th or early 19th century, allowing the gradual build-up of a headland along this line, but had gone out of use by the time the 1st edition Ordnance Survey map was drawn up in 1873.

Alternatively, the build-up of soil could have resulted from quarrying after that date. The linear north-south alignment of the gravel quarry shown on the 2nd edition O.S. map of 1900 (Plate 11) suggests that a temporary boundary on this alignment was put up when gravel extraction began, and the topsoil and subsoil from the area of the quarry may have been stripped and dumped along the west side. This would explain why the soils all contain a mixture of finds, presumably derived from earlier occupation on the site. Against this interpretation, the western edge of the quarry appeared to cut through all of the layers in the soil accumulation. It is however possible either that the quarry was extended westwards during its lifetime, or that the edge eroded or collapsed, so cutting into the edge of the dumped soils. The 3rd edition 6″ O.S. map of 1914 does show a north-south boundary along the line of the putative headland, which had disappeared by the 4th edition 6″ O.S. map of 1938, by which time the present outline of the cemetery had been established.

CONCLUDING REMARKS
by Tim Allen

The original research aims were modified as the work progressed. Although the build-up of soil down the middle of the site proved to derive not from a medieval headland but from post-medieval quarrying, and thus the hoped-for preservation of a Saxon ground surface was not forthcoming, a variety of significant new discoveries was made, leading to further research objectives, particularly as regards the Neolithic and Bronze Ages. The site has clearly had a very long history of inhabitation, and was a significant focus within the area for more than 4000 years.

The ability of the investigations to answer the research questions was hampered most by the limited area remaining for excavation by 2000; had the opportunity been taken to investigate the site sooner, significantly more of the cemetery area could have been recorded prior to destruction. For the future, small areas will remain untouched within the cemetery itself below the central walkways, providing a potential opportunity to examine more of the timber circle. The historic maps indicate that quarrying has removed any archaeological deposits over much of the area immediately east and north of the cemetery, but beyond this, private gardens on the east, south and south-east may well contain further traces of past activity. Geophysical survey has shown that an area of undisturbed archaeology still survives south-west of the cemetery, and this could add significantly to our understanding of the past history of this long-lived site.

Bibliography

Abercromby, J, 1912 *A study of the Bronze Age pottery of Great Britain and Ireland and its associated grave goods*, Oxford

Abingdon and District Archaeological Society, 1973 Abingdon: Corporation Farm, *CBA Group 9 Newsletter* **3**, 40–41

Aerts-Bijma, A T, Meijer, H A J, and van der Plicht, J, 1997 AMS sample handling in Groningen, *Nuclear Instruments and Methods in Physics Research B* **123**, 221–5

Aerts-Bijma, A T, van der Plicht, J, and Meijer, H A J, 2001 Automatic AMS sample combustion and CO_2 collection, *Radiocarbon* **43**, 293–8

Ainslie, R, 1991 Andersey Island, Abingdon, *South Midlands Archaeol* **21**, 111–114

Ainslie, R, 1992a Excavations at Thrupp near Radley, Oxon, *South Midlands Archaeol* **22**, 63–5

Ainslie, R, 1992b Abingdon: Tithe Farm, *South Midlands Archaeol* **22**, 65–8

Ainslie, R, 1995 Abingdon: 64 Bath Street, *South Midlands Archaeol* **25**, 72–4

Ainslie, R, 1999a Abingdon: Spring Road Cemetery, *South Midlands Archaeol* **29**, 29–30

Ainslie, R, 1999b Thrupp near Radley, *South Midlands Archaeol* **29**, 30–31

Ainslie, R, 2002 Abingdon, Barton lane, *South Midlands Archaeol* **32**, 36–8

Ainslie, R, and Wallis, J, 1987 Excavations on the Cursus at Drayton, Oxon, *Oxoniensia* **52**, 1–10

Akoshima, K, 1987 Microflaking quantification, in *The human uses of flint and chert* (eds G de G Sieveking and M Newcomer), Cambridge, 71–79

Allen, M, Morris, M, and Clark, R H, 1995 Food for the living: a reassessment of a Bronze Age barrow at Buckskin, Basingstoke, Hampshire, *Proc Prehist Soc* **61**, 157–189

Allen, T G, 1981 Hardwick with Yelford: Smith's Field, *CBA Group 9 Newsletter* **11**, 124–127

Allen, T G, 1990a Abingdon Vineyard redevelopment, *South Midlands Archaeol* **20**, 73–8

Allen, T G, 1990b *An Iron Age and Romano-British enclosed settlement at Watkins Farm, Northmoor, Oxon*, Thames Valley Landscapes: the Windrush Valley **1**, Oxford

Allen, T G, 1991 An *oppidum* at Abingdon, Oxfordshire, *South Midlands Archaeol* **21**, 97–9

Allen, T G, 1993a Abingdon, Abingdon Vineyard 1992: Areas 2 and 3, the early defences, *South Midlands Archaeol* **23**, 64–6

Allen, T G, 1993b South Hinksey: Hinksey Hill Farm, *South Midlands Archaeol* **23**, 77–9.

Allen, T G, 1994 Abingdon: The Vineyard, Area 3, *South Midlands Archaeol* **24**, 33–5

Allen, T G, 1995 Abingdon: The Vineyard, Area 2 watching brief, *South Midlands Archaeol* **25**, 49

Allen, T G, 1996 Abingdon Vineyard Area 6, *South Midlands Archaeol* **26**, 51–5

Allen, T G, 1997 Abingdon: West Central Redevelopment Area, *South Midlands Archaeol* **27**, 47–54

Allen, T, 2000 The Iron Age background, in *Roman Oxfordshire* (M Henig and P Booth), Stroud, 1–33

Allen, T, Miles, D, and Palmer, S, 1984 Iron Age buildings in the Upper Thames Region, in *Aspects of the Iron Age in Central Southern Britain*, (B Cunliffe and D Miles eds), Oxford University Committee for Archaeology Monograph **2**, 89–101

Allen, T G, Darvill T C, Green, L S and Jones, M U, 1993 *Excavations at Roughground Farm, Lechlade, Gloucestershire: a prehistoric and Roman landscape*, Thames Valley Landscapes: the Cotswold Water Park **1**, Oxford

Allen, T G, and Robinson, M A, 1993 *The prehistoric landscape and Iron Age enclosed settlement at Mingies Ditch, Hardwick-with-Yelford, Oxon*, Thames Valley Landscapes: the Windrush Valley **2**, Oxford

Allen, T, and Lamdin-Whymark, H, 2004 Taplow Court, Taplow, Buckinghamshire: post-excavation assessment and updated project design, Unpublished client report, prepared for English Heritage on behalf of SGI-UK, Oxford Archaeology, Oxford

Allen, T, and Lamdin-Whymark, H, 2005 Little Wittenham: excavations at and around Castle Hill, *South Midlands Archaeology* **35**, 69–82

Anderson, T, 1995 The human skeletons, in *Iron Age burials from Mill Hill, Deal*, (K Parfitt), London, 114–144

Atkinson, R J C, 1947 Notes and news, *Oxoniensia* **12**, 163

Atkinson, R J C and McKenzie, A, 1946 Notes and news, *Oxoniensia* **11**, 162

Aufderheide, A C, and Rodríguez-Martin, C, 1998, *Cambridge encyclopaedia of palaeopathology*, Cambridge

Avery, M, 1982 The Neolithic causewayed enclosure, Abingdon, in Case and Whittle 1982, 10–50

Avery, M, and Brown, D, 1972 Saxon features at Abingdon, *Oxoniensia* **37**, 66–81

Baker, S, 2002 Prehistoric and Romano-British landscapes at Little Wittenham and Long Wittenham, Oxfordshire, *Oxoniensia* **68**, 1–28

Balkwill, C, 1978 Appendix 1: a pit with Grooved Ware from Abingdon, in Parrington 1978, 31–3

Barber, M, Field, D and Topping, P, 1999 *The Neolithic flint mines of England*, Swindon

Barclay, A, 1999 Grooved Ware from the Upper Thames, in Cleal and MacSween 1999, 9–24

Barclay, A, 2006 Late Bronze Age pottery, in *The archaeology of the Wallingford Bypass, 1986–92* (A Cromarty, A J Barclay and G Lambrick) Thames Valley Landscapes

Barclay, A, Boyle, A, and Keevill, G, D, 2001 A prehistoric enclosure at Eynsham Abbey, Oxfordshire, *Oxoniensia* **66**, 105–162

Barclay, A and Edwards, E in prep. The prehistoric pottery, in Hey in prep.

Barclay, A, Gray, M, and Lambrick, G, 1995 *Excavations at the Devil's Quoits, Stanton Harcourt, Oxfordshire 1972–3 and 1988,* Thames Valley Landscapes: the Windrush Valley **3**, Oxford

Barclay, A and Halpin, C, 1999 *Excavations at Barrow Hills, Radley, Oxfordshire. Volume 1: the Neolithic and Bronze Age monuments,* Thames Valley Landscapes **11**, Oxford

Barclay, A, Lambrick, G, Moore, J and Robinson, M, 2003 *Lines in the Landscape. Cursus monuments in the Upper Thames Valley: excavations at the Drayton and Lechlade cursuses,* Thames Valley Landscapes **15**, Oxford

Barclay, A, and Lupton, A, 1999 Discussion: the early prehistoric period, in *Excavations alongside Roman Ermin Street, Gloucestershire and Wiltshire. The archaeology of the A419/A417 Swindon to Gloucester Road Scheme,* (A Mudd, R J Williams A and Lupton), Eynsham, vol. **2**, 513–517

Barrett, J, 1975 The later pottery: types, affinities, chronology and significance, in *Rams Hill: a Bronze Age Defended Enclosure and its landscape* (R Bradley and A Ellison), BAR Brit Ser **19**, Oxford

Barrett, J, 1980 The pottery of the later Bronze Age in lowland England, *Proc Prehist Soc,* **46**, 297–319

Barrett, J, 1986, The Pottery, in A Late Bronze Age riverside settlement at Wallingford, Oxfordshire (R Thomas, M Robinson, J Barrett and B Wilson), *Archaeol J* **143**, 174–200

Bass, W M, 1987 *Human osteology: A laboratory and field manual,* 3rd edn, Columbia

Bayley, J, 1999 Appendix: notes on the composition of coloured glasses, in Guido 1999, 89–93

Beavan-Athfield, N, and Sparks, R J, 2001 Bomb carbon as a tracer of dietary carbon sources in omnivorous mammals, *Radiocarbon,* **43**, 711–21

Bell, M, 1990 *Brean Down excavations, 1983–1987,* English Heritage Archaeol Rep **15**, London

Benson, D and Miles, D, 1974 *The Upper Thames Valley: an archaeological survey of the river gravels,* Oxford

Berisford, F, 1973 The early Anglo-Saxon settlement sites in the Upper Thames basin, with special reference to the area around Cassington and Eynsham, Unpublished B. Litt. thesis, University of Oxford, Oxford

Berisford, F, 1981 The Anglo-Saxon pottery, in Excavations at Beech House Hotel, Dorchester-on-Thames, 1972 (T Rowley and L Brown), *Oxoniensia* **46**, 39–43

BGS, 1971 *Geological survey of Great Britain,* Sheet **253** (*Drift*), London

Blair, J, 1994 *Anglo-Saxon Oxfordshire,* Stroud

Blinkhorn, P W, 1997 Habitus, social identity and Anglo-Saxon pottery, in Cumberpatch, and Blinkhorn (eds) 1997, 113–24

Blinkhorn, P W, 2001 The post-Roman pottery, in Excavations at the Oxford Science Park, Littlemore, Oxford (J Moore), *Oxoniensia* **66**, 163–219

Blinkhorn, P W, 2003 The pottery, in Hardy *et al.,* 159–206, 229–47

Blinkhorn, P W, 2007 Anglo-Saxon pottery, in Chambers and McAdam 2007

Boessneck, J, 1969 Osteological Differences in Sheep (*Ovis aries* Linné) and Goat (*Capra hircus* Linné), in *Science in Archaeology* (eds D Brothwell and E Higgs), London, 331–358

Booth, P 1991 Intersite comparisons between pottery assemblages in Roman Warwickshire: ceramic indicators of site status, *J Roman Pottery Studies* **4**, 1–10

Booth, P, Boyle, A and Keevill, G, 1993 A Romano-British kiln site at Lower Farm, Nuneham Courtenay, and other sites on the Didcot to Oxford and Wootton to Abingdon Water Mains, Oxfordshire, *Oxoniensia* **58**, 87–217

Booth, P, and Simmonds, A, in prep. *Appleford's earliest farmers: archaeological work at Appleford Sidings, Oxfordshire, 1993–2000,* Oxford Archaeology Occasional Papers, Oxford

Bourdillon, J, 1994 The animal provisioning of Saxon Southampton, in *Environment and economy in Anglo-Saxon England: a review of recent work on the environmental archaeology of rural and urban Anglo-Saxon settlements in England* (ed. J Rackham), C B A Res Rep **89**, London, 120–125

Bourdillon, J and Coy, J, 1980 The animal bones, in *Excavations at Melbourne Street, Southampton 1971–76,* (ed. P Holdsworth) CBA Res Rep **33**, 79–120

Boyle, A forthcoming The Iron Age human skeletal assemblage from Yarnton, in *Yarnton: Iron Age and Romano-British settlement and landscape,* (G Hey and J Timby), Thames Valley Landscapes Monograph, Oxford

Bradley, P, 1999 Worked flint, in Barclay and Halpin 1999, 211–277

Bradley, P, forthcoming The struck flint from Abingdon Vineyard, Thames Valley Landscapes monograph, Oxford

Bradley, R, 1984 Radley: Barrow Hills, the Neolithic features, *South Midlands Archaeol* **14**, 111–120

Bradley, R, 1986 The Bronze Age in the Oxford Area – its local and regional significance, in Briggs *et al.,*1986, 38–48

Brickley, M and McKinley, J, 2004 Guidelines to the standards for recording human remains, *IFA Technical Paper* **7**, Reading

Briggs, G, Cook, J and T Rowley, 1986 *The Archaeology of the Oxford Region* (eds) Oxford University Department for External Studies, Oxford

Bronk Ramsey, C, 1995 Radiocarbon calibration and analysis of stratigraphy, *Radiocarbon* **36**, 425–30

Bronk Ramsey, C, 1998 Probability and dating, *Radiocarbon* **40**, 461–74

Bronk Ramsey, C, and Hedges, R E M, 1997 A gas ion source for radiocarbon dating, *Nuclear Instruments and Methods in Physics Research* B **29**, 45–9

Bronk Ramsey, C, Higham, T F G, Hedges, R E M, forthcoming Improvements to the pretreatment of bone at Oxford, *Radiocarbon*

Brothwell, D,1981 *Digging up bones*, 3rd edn, London

Brown, P D C, 1968 Notes and news, *Oxoniensia* **33**, 137–8

Brück, J, 1999 Houses, lifestyles and deposition on middle Bronze Age settlements in southern England, *Proc Prehist Soc* **65**, 145–167

Bull, G and Payne, S, 1982 Tooth eruption and epiphyseal fusion in pigs and wild boar, in *Ageing and sexing animal bones from archaeological sites* (eds B Wilson, C Grigson and S Payne), BAR Brit Ser **109**, 55–71, Oxford

Butcher, S A, 1978 The Brooches, in, Excavations at Wakerley, Northants, 1972–75 (D A Jackson and T M Ambrose) *Britannia* **9**, 216–220

Canti, M, 2001 Geoarchaeology, in OAU 2001, 45–6

Case, H, 1956a The Neolithic causewayed camp at Abingdon, Berks, *Antiquaries Journal* **36**, 16–18

Case, H, 1956b Beaker pottery from the Oxford region, *Oxoniensia* **21**, 1–21

Case, H, 1957 Notes and news, *Oxoniensia* **22**, 104–6

Case, H J, 1982 Cassington, 1950–2: late Neolithic pits and the big enclosure, in Case and Whittle (eds) 1982, 118–151

Case, H J, 1993 Beakers: deconstruction and after, *Proc Prehist Soc* **59**, 241–68

Case, H J, Bayne, N, Steele, S, Avery, M and Sutermeister, H, 1964–5 Excavations at City Farm, Hanborough, Oxon, *Oxoniensia* **29–30**, 1–98

Case, H J and Whittle, A W R, (eds) 1982 *Settlement patterns in the Oxford region: excavations at the Abingdon causewayed enclosure and other sites*, CBA Res Rep **44**, London

Catling, H W, 1982 Six ring ditches at Standlake, in Case and Whittle 1982, 88–102

Chadwick Hawkes, S, 1986 The early Saxon period, in, Briggs *et al.* 1982, 64–113

Chambers, R, 1986 Abingdon: Ashville Trading Estate, *South Midlands Archaeology* **16**, 93

Chambers, R A and Fuller, B, 1986 Abingdon: Faringdon Road, *South Midlands Archaeology* **16**, 93

Chambers, R A and Halpin, C, 1986 Radley: Barrow Hills, *South Midlands Archaeol* **16**, 106–111

Chambers, R A and McAdam, E, 2007, *Excavations at Radly Barrow Hills, Radley, Oxfordshire.* **2**, *the Romano-British cemetery and early Anglo-Saxon settlement*, Thames Valley Landscapes, **25**, Oxford

Chaplin, R E, 1971 *The study of animal bones from archaeological sites*, London

Chisholm, B S, Nelson, D E, and Schwarcz, H P, 1982 Stable carbon isotope ratios as a measure of marine versus terrestrial protein in ancient diets, *Science* **216**, 1131–32

Clapham, A R, Tutin, T G and Moore, D M, 1987 *Flora of the British Isles*, 3rd edn, Cambridge

Clarke, D L, 1970 *Beaker pottery of Great Britain and Ireland*, Cambridge

Clarke, D V, Cowie, T G, and Foxon, A, 1985 *Symbols of power*, Edinburgh

Cleal, R M J, 1990 The prehistoric pottery, in Richards 1990, 45–57

Cleal, R M J, 1999 Prehistoric Pottery, in Barclay and Halpin eds 1999, 195–210

Cleal, R, with Case, H and Barclay, A, 2003 Neolithic and Bronze Age pottery, in Barclay *et al.* 2003, 135–148

Cleal, R and MacSween, A, 1999 *Grooved Ware in Great Britain and Ireland*, Neolithic Studies Group Seminar Papers **3**, Oxford

Clutton-Brock, J, 1979 The Animal Resources, in *The archaeology of Anglo-Saxon England* (ed. D M Wilson), London, 373 – 392

Cohen, A, and Serjeantson, D, 1996 *A manual for the identification of bird bones from archaeological sites*, 2nd edn, London

Cotterell, B, and Kamminga, J, 1979 The mechanics of flint flaking, in *Lithic use-wear analysis* (ed. B Hayden), London

Cox, M, 1989 *The story of Abingdon, part II: medieval Abingdon, 1186–1556*, Abingdon

Coy, J, 1982 The role of wild vertebrate fauna in urban economies in Wessex, in *Environmental archaeology in the urban context* (eds A R Hall and H K Edward), C B A Res Rep **43**, London, 107–116

Coy, J, 1989, The provision of fowls and fish for town, in *Diet and crafts in towns: the evidence of animal remains from the Roman to the post-medieval periods* (eds D Serjeantson and T Waldron), BAR Brit Ser **199**, London, 25–40

Crabtree, P J, 1994 Animal exploitation in East-Anglian villages, in *Environment and economy in Anglo-Saxon England* (ed. J Rackham), CBA Res Rep **89**, London, 40–54

Cumberpatch, C G, and Blinkhorn, P W, (eds) 1997 *Not so much a pot, more a way of life* Oxbow Monograph **83**, Oxford

Cunliffe, B, 1984 *Danebury: an Iron Age hillfort in Hampshire, vol 2. The Excavations 1969–1978: the finds*, CBA Res Rep **52**, London

Cunliffe, B, 2000 *The Danebury environs programme: the prehistory of a Wessex Landscape, vol. 1: introduction*, English Heritage and OUCA Monograph **48**, Oxford

Cunliffe, B and Poole, C, 2000 *Suddern Farm, Middle Wallop, Hants, 1991 and 1996. The Danebury environs programme: the prehistory of a Wessex landscape*, English Heritage and OUCA Monograph **49**, Oxford

Dawes, J, nd Wetwang Slack human bone report, Unpublished MS

De Roche, C, 1978, The Iron Age pottery, in Parrington 1978, 40–74

De Roche, C, and Lambrick G, 1980, The Iron Age pottery, in Hinchcliffe and Thomas 1980, 45–59

Dehling, H and van der Plicht, J 1993 Statistical problems in calibrating radiocarbon dates, *Radiocarbon* **35**, 239

Dewey, H, and Bromehead, C E N, 1915 *The geology of the country around Windsor and Chertsey*, Mem Geol Survey, London

Donaldson, P, 1977 The excavation of a multiple round barrow at Barnack, Cambridgeshire, 1974–76, *Proc Soc Antiq Lond* **57**, 197–231

Driesch, A von den, 1976 *A guide to the measurements of animal bones from archaeological sites*, Peabody Museum of Archaeology and Ethnology Bulletin **1**, Harvard

Dunham, K C, 1971 *Geological survey of Great Britain, sheet 253, (Drift)*, London

Ehrenberg, M, Price, J, and Vale, V, 1982 The excavation of two Bronze Age round barrows at Welsh St. Donats, South Glamorgan, *Bulletin of the Board of Celtic Studies, 29(4)*, 831

Evans, J, 2001 Material approaches to the identification of different Romano-British site types, in *Britons and Romans: advancing an archaeological agenda* (eds S James and M Millett), CBA Res Rep **125**, London, 26–35

Everett, R N and Eeles, B M G, 1999 Investigations at Thrupp House Farm, Radley, near Abingdon, *Oxoniensia* **64**, 117–152

Fell, C, 1936, The Hunsbury Hillfort, Northants, *Archaeol J* **93**, 57–100

Fitzpatrick, A P, 1997 Everyday life in Iron Age Wessex, in *Reconstructing Iron Age Societies: new approaches to the British Iron Age*, (eds A Gwilt and C Haselgrove), Oxbow Monograph **71**, Oxford, 73–86

Ford, S, 1987 Chronological and functional aspects of flint assemblages, in *Lithic analysis and later British prehistory* (eds A G Brown and M R Edmonds), BAR Brit Ser **162**, Oxford, 67–81

Ford, S, with Entwistle, R, and Taylor, K 2003 *Excavations at Cippenham, Slough, Berkshire, 1995–7*, Thames Valley Archaeological Services Monograph **3**, Reading

Foster, J, 1990 Other Bronze Age artefacts, in Bell, 1990, 158–175

Frere, S S, 1984 Excavations at Dorchester-on-Thames, 1963, *Archaeol J* **141**, 91–174

Garwood, P, 1999 Grooved Ware chronology, in Cleal and MacSween 1999, 145–176

Gibbs, A V, 1989 Sex, gender and material culture patterning in later Neolithic and Early Bronze Age England, Unpublished PhD thesis, University of Cambridge, Cambridge

Gibson, A, 1998 *Stonehenge and timber circles*, Stroud

Gingell C J, and Morris E, 2000, Pottery: form series, in Lawson 2000, 149–77

Gledhill, A and Wallis, J, 1989 Sutton Courtenay: a Neolithic long enclosure, *South Midlands Archaeol* **19**, 58–9

Goodman, A H, Armelagos, G J, and Rose, J C, 1980 Enamel hypoplasias as indicators of stress in three prehistoric populations from Illinois, *Human Biology* **52**, 515–528

Goodman, A H, and Rose, J C, 1990 Assessment of systemic physiological perturbations from dental enamel hypoplasias and associated histological structures, *Yearbook of Physical Anthropology* **33**, 59–110

Grant, A, 1982 The use of tooth wear as a guide to the age of domestic ungulates, in Wilson *et al.* 1982, 91–108

Gray, M, 1972 Notes and news, *Oxoniensia* **37**, 238–241

Green, M, 2000 *A landscape revealed: 10,000 years on a chalkland farm*, Stroud

Grigson, C, 1982 Sex and age determination of some bones and teeth of domestic cattle: a review of the literature, in Wilson *et al. 1982*, 155–206

Grimes, W F, 1960 *Excavations on defence sites, 1939–1945*, **1**: *mainly Neolithic-Bronze Age*, Ministry of Works Archaeol Rep **3**, London

Guido, M, 1978 *The glass beads of the prehistoric and Roman periods in Britain and Ireland*, Rep Res Comm Soc Antiq Lond **35**, London

Guido, M, (ed. M. Welch) 1999 *The glass beads of Anglo-Saxon England c AD 400–700: a preliminary visual classification of the more definite and diagnostic types*, Rep Res Comm Soc Antiq Lond **58**, London

Hall, M, 1992, The prehistoric pottery, in Moore and Jennings 1992, 63–82

Halpin, C, 1983 Abingdon: Ex-MG car factory site, *South Midlands Archaeol* **13**, 113–114

Halstead, P, 1985 A study of mandibular teeth from Romano-British contexts at Maxey, in *Archaeology and environment in the Lower Welland Valley 1* (F Pryor and C French), East Anglian Archaeology Report **27**, Norwich, 219–224

Hambleton, E, 1999 *Animal husbandry regimes in Iron Age Britain: a comparative study of faunal assemblages from British Iron Age sites*, BAR British Series **282**, Oxford

Hamerow, H F, 1993 *Excavations at Mucking volume* **2**, *the Anglo-Saxon settlement*, English Heritage Archaeol Rep **21**, London

Hamerow, H F, Hayden, C and Hey, G, in prep. Anglo-Saxon and earlier settlement at Drayton Road, Sutton Courtenay

Hammond, P W, 1993, *Food and feast in medieval England*, Stroud

Harding, D W, 1972 *The Iron Age in the Upper Thames basin*, Oxford

Harding, D W, 1987 *Excavations in Oxfordshire 1964–66*, University of Edinburgh Occasional Paper **15**, Edinburgh

Harding, P, 1990 The worked flint, in Richards 1990, *passim*

Hardy, A, Dodd, A and Keevill, G D, 2003 *Aelfric's Abbey: excavations at Eynsham Abbey, Oxfordshire, 1989–92*, Thames Valley Landscapes **16**, Oxford

Harman, M 2004 Human and animal bone, in Lambrick and Allen 2004 457–463

Harman, M and Wilson, B, 1981 A Medieval graveyard beside Faringdon Road, Abingdon, *Oxoniensia* **46**, 56–61

Healy, F, 2005 Discussion of the penannular post-ring, in Lambrick and Allen 2004, 62–63

Healy, F, Heaton, M and Lobb, S J, 1992 Excavations of a Mesolithic site at Thatcham, Berkshire, *Proc Prehist Soc* **58**, 41–76

Hearne, C M, 2000 Archaeological evaluation in the Vale of White Horse, near Abingdon, *Oxoniensia* **65**, 7–12

Henig, M and Booth, P, 2000 *Roman Oxfordshire*, Stroud

Hey, G, 1993 Yarnton floodplain, *South Midlands Archaeol* **9**, 82–85

Hey, G, 1995 Iron Age and Roman settlements at Old Shifford Farm, Standlake, *Oxoniensia* **60**, 93–175

Hey, G, in prep. *Yarnton: Neolithic and Bronze Age settlement and landscape*, Thames Valley Landscapes, Oxford

Hey, G, Bayliss, A, and Boyle, A, 1999 A Middle Iron Age inhumation cemetery at Yarnton, Oxfordshire, *Antiquity* **73**, 551–62

Higham, C F W, 1967 Stock rearing as a cultural factor in Prehistoric Europe, *Proceedings of the Prehistoric Society* **33**, 84–106

Hiller, J, and Allen, T, 2001 Abingdon Spring Road Cemetery, *South Midlands Archaeology* **31**, 55–58

Hillson, S, 1996 *Dental anthropology*, Cambridge

Hinchcliffe, J, and Thomas R, 1980, Archaeological investigations at Appleford, *Oxoniensia* **45**, 18–73

Hingley, R, 1980, Excavations by R A Rutland on an Iron Age site at Wittenham Clumps, *Berkshire Archaeol J* **70** (1979–80), 21–55

Hingley, R, and Miles, D, 1984 Aspects of the Iron Age in the Upper Thames Valley, in *Aspects of the Iron Age in Central Southern Britain* (eds B Cunliffe and D Miles), University of Oxford Committee for Archaeology Monograph **2**, 52–71

Holgate, R, 1986 Mesolithic, Neolithic and earlier Bronze Age settlement patterns south-west of Oxford, *Oxoniensia* **51**, 1–14

Holgate, R, 1988 Neolithic settlement of the Thames Basin, BAR Brit Ser **194**, Oxford

Hooper, B, 1984 Anatomical considerations, in Cunliffe 1984, 463–74

Hooper, B, 2000 The cemetery population, in Cunliffe and Poole 2000, 168–170

Hunter, A G, and Kirk, J R, 1952/53 Excavations at Campsfield, Kidlington, Oxon, 1949, *Oxoniensia* **17/18**, 36–62

Inizan, M-L, Roche, H and Tixier, J, 1992 *Technology of knapped stone*, Meudon

Jones, G 1983 Abingdon: 6 Lombard Street, *South Midlands Archaeol* **13**, 113

Juel Jensen, H, 1994 *Flint tools and plant working: hidden traces of Stone Age technology*, Aarhus

Keevill, G D, 1992 An Anglo-Saxon site at Audlett Drive, Abingdon, Oxon., *Oxoniensia* **57**, 55–79

Lacaille, A D, 1937 Prehistoric pottery found at Iver, Bucks, *Rec Buckinghamshire* **13**, 287–99

Lambot, B, 2000 Victimes, sacrificateurs et dieux, *L'Archaeologue* Hors Serie **2**, 30–36

Lambrick, G, 1979, The Iron Age pottery, in Lambrick and Robinson 1979, 35–46

Lambrick, G, 1992 The development of late Prehistoric and Roman farming on the Thames gravels, in *Developing landscapes of Lowland Britain. The archaeology of the British gravels: a review* (eds M Fulford

and E Nichols), Soc Antiq Lond Occasional Paper **14**, 78–105

Lambrick, G, and Allen, T G, 2004 *Gravelly Guy, Stanton Harcourt, Oxfordshire: the development of a prehistoric and Romano-British landscape*, Thames Valley Landscapes **21**, Oxford

Lambrick, G, and Robinson, M, 1979, *Iron Age and Roman riverside settlements at Farmoor, Oxfordshire*, Oxford Archaeol Unit Rep 2/CBA Res Rep **32**, Oxford and London

Lambrick, G, and Slade, C F, 1991 *Two cartularies of Abingdon Abbey* **II**, *Chatsworth Cartulary*, Oxford Historical Society New Series **33**, London

Lamdin-Whymark, H, forthcoming The struck flint, in *The archaeology of a Middle Thames landscape: The Eton rowing course at Dorney lake and the Maidenhead, Eton and Windsor flood alleviation channel*, **1**, *the early prehistoric landscape* (T G Allen, and A J Barclay), Thames Valley Landscapes, Oxford

Lawson, A J, 2000 *Potterne 1982–5: animal husbandry in later prehistoric Wiltshire*, Wessex Archaeology Report **17**, Salisbury

Leeds, E T, 1929 Bronze Age urns from Long Wittenham, *Antiq. J* **9**, 153–4

Leeds, E T, 1934 Recent Bronze Age discoveries in Berkshire and Oxon, *Antiq J* **14**, 264–76

Leeds, E T, 1947 A Saxon village at Sutton Courtney, Berkshire, third report, *Archaeologia* **92**, 79–95

Leeds, E T and Harden, D B, 1936 *The Anglo-Saxon cemetery at Abingdon, Berkshire*, Oxford

Longley, D, with Needham, S, 1980 *Runnymede Bridge 1976: excavations on the site of a Late Bronze Age settlement*, Surrey Archaeological Society Research **6**, Guildford

Longworth, I H, 1983 The Whinny Liggate perforated wallcup and its affinities, in *From the stone age to the 'forty five* .(eds A O'Connor and D V Clarke), Edinburgh, 65–86

Lovejoy, C O, Meindl, R S, Pryzbeck, T R, and Mensforth, R P, 1985 Chronological metamorphosis of the auricular surface of the illium: a new method for determination of adult skeletal age-at-death, *American Journal of Physical Anthropology* **68**, 15–28

Lyman, R L, 1996 *Vertebrate taphonomy*, Cambridge

Mallouf, R J, 1982 An analysis of plow-damaged chert artefacts: the Brookeen Creek cache, Hill County, Texas, *J Field Archaeology* **9**, 79–98

Manby, T, 1995 Neolithic and Bronze Age pottery, in *The excavation of seven Bronze Age barrows on the moorlands of north-east Yorkshire*. (T C M Brewster and A E Finney), Yorkshire Archaeological Report **1**

Masters, P M, 1987 Preferential preservation of non-collagenous protein during bone diagenesis: implications for chronometric and stable isotope measurements, *Geochimica et Cosmochimica Acta*, **51**, 3209–14

Mays, S, 2000 Stable isotope analysis in ancient human skeletal remains in *Human osteology in archaeology and forensic science* (eds M Cox and S Mays), London, 425–438

McCarthy, M R, and Brooks, C M, 1988 *Medieval pottery in Britain AD 900–1600*, Leicester

Meadows, K I, 1997 Much ado about nothing: the social context of eating and drinking in early Roman Britain, in Cumberpatch and Blinkhorn 1997, 21–36

Mellor, M, 1980 The Pottery, in A Beaker burial and medieval tenements in The Hamel, Oxford (N Palmer), *Oxoniensia* 45, 124–255

Mellor, M, 1994 Oxford Pottery: a synthesis of middle and late Saxon, medieval and early post-medieval pottery in the Oxford Region, *Oxoniensia* 59, 17–217

Mercer, R J, 1981 The excavation of a late Neolithic henge-type enclosure at Balfarg, Markinch, Fife, Scotland, 1977–8 *Proc Soc Antiq Scot* 111, 63–171

Miles, D, 1975 Excavations at West St Helen Street, Abingdon, *Oxoniensia* 40, 79–101

Miles, D, 1977 Appendix 2. Cropmarks around Northfield Farm, in Northfield Farm, Long Wittenham (M Gray), *Oxoniensia* 42, 24–9

Miles, D, 1984 *Archaeology at Barton Court Farm, Abingdon, Oxon*, Oxford Archaeological Unit Rep 3, CBA Res Rep 50, London

Mook, W G, 1986 Business meeting: recommendations/resolutions adopted by the Twelfth International Radiocarbon Conference, *Radiocarbon* 28, 799

Moore, H L 1982 The interpretation of spatial patterning in settlement residues, in *Symbolic and structural archaeology* (ed. I Hodder), Cambridge, 74–9

Moore, J, and Jennings, D, 1992, *Reading Business Park: a Bronze Age landscape*, Thames Valley Landscapes: the Kennet Valley 1, Oxford

Moss, E H, 1983 Some comments on edge damage as a factor in functional analysis of stone artefacts, *J Archaeol Sci* 10, 231–242

Mudd, A, 1995 The excavation of a late Bronze Age/early Iron Age site at Eight Acre Field, Radley, *Oxoniensia* 60, 21–65

Muir, J and Roberts, M, 1999 *Excavations at Wyndyke Furlong, Abingdon, Oxfordshire, 1994*, Thames Valley Landscapes 12, Oxford

Musson, C, 1970 House plans and prehistory, *Current Archaeology* 21, 367–77

Myres, J N L, 1968 The Anglo-Saxon cemetery, in The early history of Abingdon, Berkshire, and its abbey (M Biddle, H T Lambrick and J N L Myres), *Medieval Archaeol* 12, 35–41

Myres, J N L, 1977 *A corpus of Anglo-Saxon pottery of the pagan period*, Cambridge

Needham, S, 1996 Chronology and periodisation in the British Bronze Age, *Acta Archaeologia* 67, 121–40

Needham, S, and Ambers, J, 1994 Redating Rams Hill and reconsidering Bronze Age enclosure, *Proc Prehist Soc* 60, 225– 243

Northover, J P, 1999a The earliest metalworking in southern Britain, in *The beginnings of metallurgy* (eds A Hauptmann, E Pernicka, T Rehren and Ü Yalçin), Deutsches Bergbau-Museum Beiheft 9, Bochum, 211–226

Northover, J P, 1999b Analysis of early Bronze Age metalwork from Barrow Hills, in Barclay and Halpin 1999, 192–5

OA 2005 British Gas Site, the Vineyard and Penlon Site, Radley Road, Abingdon, Oxon: post-excavation assessment and updated project design, Unpublished client report prepared on behalf of Kings Oak, Oxford Archaeology, Oxford

OAU, 1990 Abingdon Spring Road Cemetery, 1990: archaeological evaluation, Unpublished report for English Heritage, Oxford Archaeology, Oxford

OAU, 1992 Oxford Archaeological Unit field manual, Unpublished MSS, Oxford Archaeology, Oxford

OAU, 1997 Abingdon Multiplex, Abingdon, Oxon: archaeological evaluation report, Unpublished report for Discovery Properties Ltd and Vale of White Horse District Council, Oxford Archaeology, Oxford

OAU, 1998 Abingdon Abbey Gardens and Abbey Meadows: historical restoration management plan, appendices 1–4, Unpublished report for Vale of White Horse District Council and Heritage Lottery, Oxford Archaeology, Oxford

OAU, 2000 Abingdon, Spring Road Cemetery, fieldwork research design, Unpublished report for English Heritage, Oxford Archaeology, Oxford

OAU, 2001 Abingdon, Spring Road Cemetery: post-excavation assessment and research design, Unpublished report for English Heritage, Oxford Archaeology, Oxford

Onhuma, K and Bergman, C, 1982 Experimental studies in the determination of flake mode, *Bulletin of the Institute of Archaeology, London* 19, 161–171

Oswald, A, 1997 A doorway on the past: practical and mystic concerns in the orientation of roundhouse doorways, *Reconstructing Iron Age societies: new approaches to the British Iron Age* (eds A Gwilt and C Haselgrove), Oxbow Monograph 71, Oxford, 87–95

Parfitt, K 1995 *Iron Age burials from Mill Hill, Deal*, London

Parker, A, 1999 The pollen and sediments of Daisy Bank Fen, in Barclay and Halpin, 254–267

Parrington, M, 1978 *The excavation of an Iron Age settlement, Bronze Age ring-ditches and Roman features at Ashville Trading Estate, Abingdon (Oxfordshire) 1974–76*, CBA Res Rep 28, London

Payne, S, 1973 Kill-off patterns in sheep and goats: the mandibles from Asvan Kale, Anatolian *Studies* 23, 281–303

PCRG 1997, *The study of later prehistoric pottery: general policies and guidelines for analysis and publication*, Prehistoric Ceramics Research Group Occas pap 1–2 (rev. edn), Oxford

Pearce, J, and Vince, A, 1988 *A dated type-series of London medieval pottery. Part 4: Surrey Whitewares,*

London and Middlesex Archaeol Soc Special Paper **10**, London

Pelling, R and Robinson, M A, 2000 Saxon emmer wheat from the Upper and Middle Thames Valley, England, *Environmental Archaeology* **5**, 117–19

Piggott, S, 1962 *The West Kennet long barrow, excavations 1955–56,* Ministry of Works Archaeol Rep **4**, London

Poole, C, 1984, Objects of baked clay, in Cunliffe 1984, 398–406

Prummel, W and Frisch, H-J, 1986 A guide for the distinction of species, sex and body size in bones of sheep and goat, *Journal of Archaeological Science* **13**, 567–77

Pryor, F, 2001 *Seahenge: new discoveries in prehistoric Britain*, London

Rahtz, P, 1976 Buildings and rural settlement, in *The archaeology of Anglo-Saxon England* (ed. D M Wilson), Cambridge, 49–98

Rawes, B, 1981 The Romano-British site at Brockworth, Glos, *Britannia* **2**, 45–77

Reynolds, P, 1974 Experimental Iron Age pits: an interim report, *Proc Prehist Soc* **40**, 118–131

Rice, P M, 1987 *Pottery analysis: a sourcebook*, Chicago

Richards, J, 1990, *The Stonehenge environs project*, English Heritage Archaeol Rep **16**, London

Richardson, K M, 1951, An Iron Age site on the Chilterns, *Antiq J* **31**, 1 32–48

Richmond, I 1968 *Hod Hill: excavations carried out between 1951 and 1955 for the Trustees of the British Museum* **2**, London

Roberts, C and Cox, M 2003 *Health and disease in Britain from prehistory to the present day* Stroud

Roberts, C and Manchester, K 1995 *The archaeology of disease*, 2nd edn, New York

Robinson, M, 1999 The prehistoric environmental sequence of the Barrow Hills area, in Barclay and Halpin 1999, 269–274

Robinson, M A, 2000 Further considerations of Neolithic charred cereals, fruit and nuts, in *Plants in Neolithic Britain and beyond* (ed. A Fairbairn), Oxford, 85–90

Robinson, M A and Wilson, R, 1987 A survey of environmental archaeology in the South Midlands, in *Environmental archaeology: a regional review* **2** (ed. H C M Keeley), Historic Buildings and Monuments Commission Occasional Paper **1**, London, 16–100

Rodwell, K A (ed.), 1975 *Historic towns in Oxfordshire: a survey of the new county*, Oxfordshire Archaeological Unit Survey **3**, Oxford

Rozanski, K, Stichler, W, Gonfiantini, R, Scott, E M, Beukens, R P, Kromer, B, and van der Plicht, J, 1992 The IAEA ^{14}C intercomparison exercise 1990, *Radiocarbon* **34**, 506–19

Russell, 1973, *Soil conditions and plant growth*, London

Saville, A, 1980 On the measurement of struck flakes and flake tools, *Lithics* **1**, 16–20

Scheuer, L, Musgrave, J H and Evans, S P, 1980 The estimation of late foetal and perinatal age from limb bone length by linear and logarithmic regression, *Annals of Human Biology* **7/3**, 257–265

Schultz, P D and McHenry, H M, 1975 Age distributions of enamel hypoplasia in prehistoric California Indians, *J of Dental Research* **54**, 913

Scott, E M, Harkness, D D, and Cook, G T, 1998 Inter-laboratory comparisons: lessons learned, *Radiocarbon*, **40**, 331–40

Seager Smith, R, 2000 Worked bone and antler, in Lawson 2000, 222–240

Serjeantson, D, 1996 The animal bones, in *Runnymede Bridge research excavations, vol 2: refuse and disposal behaviour at Area 16, East Runnymede* (eds S Needham and T Spence), London, 194–233

Shand, P, Henderson, E, Henderson, R and Barclay, A, 2003 Corporation Farm, Wilsham Road, Abingdon: a summary of the Neolithic and Bronze Age excavations, 1971–4, in Barclay *et al.* 2003, 31–40

Silver, I A, 1969 The Ageing of domestic animals, in *Science in Archaeology* (eds D Brothwell and E Higgs), London, 283–302

Skellington, W A, 1978 The worked flints, in Parrington 1978, 90–91

Skellington, W, 1972 Abingdon Cemetery, *CBA Group 9 Newsletter* **2**, 22–3

Stead, I M, 1991 *Iron Age cemeteries in East Yorkshire*, English Heritage Archaeol Rep **22**, London

Stuart-Macadam, P 1991 Anaemia in Roman Britain, in *Health in past societies* (eds H Bush and M Zvelebil), BAR Int Ser **567**, Oxford, 101–113

Stuiver, M, and Kra, R S, 1986 Editorial comment, *Radiocarbon* **28**, ii

Stuiver, M, and Polach, H A, 1977 Reporting of ^{14}C data, *Radiocarbon* **19**, 355–63

Stuiver, M, and Reimer, P J, 1986 A computer program for radiocarbon age calculation, *Radiocarbon* **28**, 1022–30

Stuiver, M, and Reimer, P J, 1993 Extended ^{14}C data base and revised CALIB 3.0 ^{14}C age calibration program, *Radiocarbon* **35**, 215–30

Stuiver, M, Reimer, P J, Bard, E, Beck, J W, Burr, G S, Hughen K A, Kromer, B, McCormac, G, van der Plicht, J, and Spurk, M, 1998 INTCAL98 Radiocarbon age calibration, 24,000–0 cal BP, *Radiocarbon* **40**, 1041–83

Suchey, J M and Brooks, S 1990 Skeletal age determination based on the *os pubis*: a comparison of the Acsádi-Nemeskéri and Suchey-Brooks method, *Human Evolution* **5**, 227–238

Thomas, J, 1999 *Understanding the Neolithic*, London

Thomas, N, 1955 Excavations at Vicarage Field, Stanton Harcourt, 1951, *Oxoniensia* **20**, 1–28

Thomas, R, 1979 Roman Abingdon: an assessment of the evidence, Unpublished BA dissertation, Univ. of Southampton, Southampton

Timby, J, 1999 The Pottery, in Muir and Roberts 1999, 30–40

Tomber, R, and Dore J, 1998, *The national Roman fabric reference collection: a handbook*, London

Tringham, R, Cooper, G, Odell, G, Voytek, B, and Whitman, A, 1974 Experimentation in the formation of edge damage: a new approach to lithic analysis, *J Field Archaeology* **1**, 171–196

Trotter, M, and Gleser, G C, 1952 Estimation of stature from long bones of American Whites and Negroes, *Amer J of Physical Anthrop* **10**, 463–514

Trotter, M, and Gleser, G C, 1958 A re-evaluation of estimation of stature based on measurements of stature taken during life and long bones after death, *Amer J of Physical Anthrop* **16**, 79–123

Tuross, N, Fogel, M L, and Hare, P E, 1988 Variability in the preservation of the isotopic composition of collagen from fossil bone, *Geochimica Cosmochimica Acta* **52**, 929–35

Underwood-Keevill, C, 1992 The pottery, in An Anglo-Saxon site at Audlett Drive, Abingdon, Oxon. (G D Keevill), *Oxoniensia* **57**, 67–73

Unger-Hamilton, R, 1988 *Method in microwear analysis: prehistoric sickles and other stone tools from Arjoune, Syria*, BAR Int Ser **435**, Oxford

Van Beek, G 1983 *Dental morphology: an illustrated guide*, 2nd edn, Bristol

van der Plicht, J, Wijma, S, Aerts, A T, Pertuisot, M H, and Meijer, H A J, 2000 Status report: the Groningen AMS facility, *Nuclear Instruments and Methods in Physics Research B* **172**, 58–65

Von den Driesch, A, 1976 *A guide to the measurement of animal bones from archaeological sites*, Peabody Museum Bulletin **1**, Harvard

Wainwright G J, 1979, *Gussage All Saints: an Iron Age settlement in Dorset*, DoE Archaeol Rep **10**, London

Wainwright, G J and Longworth, I H, 1971 *Durrington Walls: excavations 1966–1968*, Rep Res Comm Soc Antiq London **29**, London

Wallis, J, 1981 Radley: Thrupp Farm, *South Midlands Archaeol* **11**, 134–7

Ward, G K, and Wilson, S R, 1978 Procedures for comparing and combining radiocarbon age determinations: a critique, *Archaeometry* **20**, 19–31

West, S, 1985 *West Stow: the Anglo-Saxon village* **1**, East Anglian Archaeol **24**, Norwich

West, S, 2001 *West Stow revisited*, West Stow

Whimster, R, 1981 *Burial practices in Iron Age Britain: a discussion and gazetteer of the evidence c 700 BC–AD 43*, BAR Brit. Ser. **90**, Oxford

Whittle, A, 1997 *Sacred mound, holy rings. Silbury Hill and the West Kennet palisade enclosures: a later Neolithic complex in north Wiltshire*, Oxbow Monograph **74**, Oxford

Whittle, A, Atkinson, R J C, Chambers, R, and Thomas, N, 1992 Excavations in the Neolithic and Bronze Age complex at Dorchester-on-Thames, Oxfordshire, 1947–1952 and 1981, *Proc Prehist Soc* **58**, 143–201

Williams, A, 1946–7 Excavations at Langford Downs, Oxon (near Lechlade), *Oxoniensia* **11–12**, 44–64

Williams, A, 1951, Excavations at Beard Mill, Stanton Harcourt, 1944, *Oxoniensia* **16**, 5–22

Wilson, R, 1978 The Animal bones, in Parrington 1978, 110 –139

Wilson, D, 1979 Inhumations and Roman settlement features at Box Hill, Abingdon, Oxon, *Oxoniensia* **44**, 97–9

Wilson, R, 1984 Faunal remains: animal bones and marine shells, in Miles (ed.) 1984, 8:A1–8:O9

Wilson, B, Grigson, C and Payne, S (eds), 1982 *Ageing and Sexing Animal Bones from Archaeological Sites*, BAR Brit Ser **109**, Oxford

Wilson, R and Wallis, J, 1991 Prehistoric activity, early Roman building, tenement yards and gardens behind Twickenham House, Abingdon, *Oxoniensia* **56**, 1–15

Workshop of European Anthropologists, 1980 Recommendations for age and sex diagnoses of infant skeletons, *Journal of Human Evolution* **9**, 517–4

Yalden, D, 1999 *The history of British mammals*, London

Yates, D T, 1999 Bronze Age field systems in the Thames Valley, *Oxford J Archaeol* **18/2**, 157–170

York, J, 2002 The life cycle of Bronze Age metalwork from the Thames, *Oxford J Archaeol* **21/1**, 77–92.

Young, C J, 1977, *Oxfordshire Roman pottery*, BAR Brit Ser **43**, Oxford

Zondervan, A, and Sparks, R J, 1997 Development plans for the AMS facility at the Institute of Geological and Nuclear Sciences, New Zealand, *Nuclear Instruments and Methods in Physics Research B* **123**, 79–83

Index